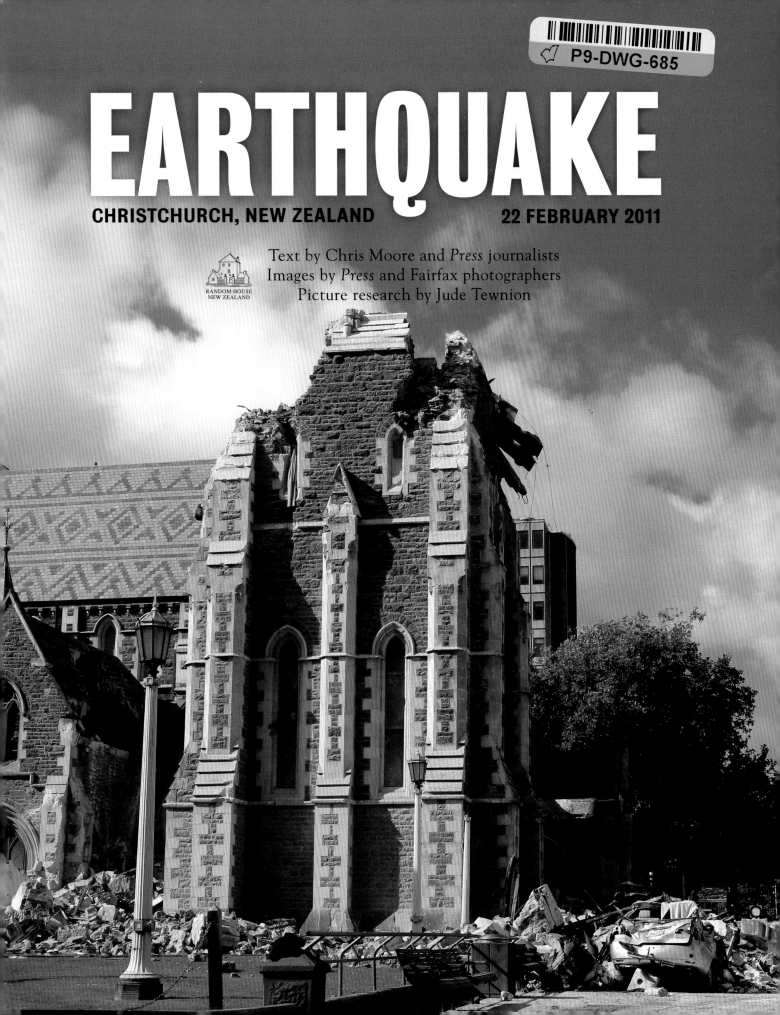

P9-DWG-685

EARTHQUAKE

CHRISTCHURCH, NEW ZEALAND   **22 FEBRUARY 2011**

RANDOM HOUSE
NEW ZEALAND

Text by Chris Moore and *Press* journalists
Images by *Press* and Fairfax photographers
Picture research by Jude Tewnion

A RANDOM HOUSE BOOK published by Random House New Zealand
18 Poland Road, Glenfield, Auckland, New Zealand

For more information about our titles go to www.randomhouse.co.nz

A catalogue record for this book is available from the National Library of New Zealand

Random House New Zealand is part of the Random House Group
New York   London   Sydney   Auckland   Delhi   Johannesburg

First published 2011

© 2011 *The Press*

The moral rights of the author have been asserted

ISBN 978 1 86979 699 0

This book is copyright. Except for the purposes of fair reviewing no part of this publication may
be reproduced or transmitted in any form or by any means, electronic or mechanical, including
photocopying, recording or any information storage and retrieval system, without permission in
writing from the publisher.

Design: Sharon Grace
Front cover images: main photograph, Iain McGregor; below from left, Carys Monteath,
    Carys Monteath, Richard Cosgrove, Colin Smith
Back cover image: Don Scott
Printed in New Zealand by Printlink in association with Rainbow Print

This publication is printed on paper pulp sourced from sustainably grown and managed forests,
using Elemental Chlorine Free (EFC) bleaching, and printed with 100% vegetable based inks.

Contents

*This book is dedicated to the memory of our colleague, Adrienne Lindsay,
and all those who died in the 22 February quake.*

Preface
Joe Bennett

Ten kilometres below the Port Hills, some rock shifted. Ten kilometres isn't far, the distance from Cathedral Square to Mt Pleasant, say, or to New Brighton, but no human being has ever travelled those 10km. Nor has sunlight. There is nothing down there to tell night from day or one century from another.

The rock shifted only a metre or two. In geophysical terms it was little more than a shrug, one of the countless tiny movements that the crust of the earth has to make to accommodate the vast forces at work on it. But the shift released substantial quantities of energy.

Twenty seconds later that energy had changed the course of maybe half a million human lives. For many this change of course was just a minor swerve. For others it was drastic, a fierce wrench of the wheel. And for a couple of hundred it was the end of the road. They were dead.

Recently I asked half a dozen people what they were doing when the quake struck. At lunchtime on a weekday a city is host to every human activity from making love to making money, so these six are not representative. But in their variety they are perhaps typical.

One was playing golf, one fetching tools near the Bridge of Remembrance, one on his back underneath a car, one on the toilet at home, one in a legal office near the CBD and one at work as a veterinary nurse.

The golfer had just played an eight-iron to the green. It was, he thought, quite a good shot. But then the fairway heaved 'like a whale's belly' and he fell over. He never found out where his ball landed.

The tradesman at the Bridge of Remembrance watched Cashel Mall fall. Then he stepped in to help. He saw sights he is reluctant to describe. He isn't sure how long he stayed, but he helped free several people from the rubble before the emergency services assumed control. It took him five hours to drive the 10km home.

The mechanic who was under the car stayed under the car. Then he went home to find his house ruined. He and his family had only lived there since the September quake, which had

What happened in those first few hours and days we now know. But at the time, those affected knew little. Power was out to most of the city, and people simply coped with what was in front of them.

ruined their previous house. His wife and kids have now gone to Invercargill and he plans to join them there soon.

'Are you coming back?' I asked.

'No, mate,' he said. 'The missus has had enough.'

The woman on the toilet took shelter under the door frame with her knickers round her ankles. She heard her chimney collapse into the hearth.

The woman in the legal office knelt under her desk. Her computer monitor fell and dangled beside her. When it stopped swinging she left the building by the main door, gawped briefly at the ruins of the Provincial Chambers, then went to find her car.

The veterinary nurse watched a miniature dachshund on the floor of the surgery. It was bouncing up and down, she said, actually leaving the floor. She threw herself on the dog and clung to it until the quake stopped.

And when it stopped, everything had changed. What had seemed important at 12.50pm did not seem important at 12.52. People were thrown back on instincts as old as our species. Survival first. Then going to the help of others. Then family. The buckled roads became choked with people trying to get to children, partners, parents.

What happened in those first few hours and days we now know. But at the time, those affected knew little. Power was out to most of the city, and people simply coped with what was in front of them.

Most of the north and west of the city got off lightly. But in the low-lying east the ground had liquefied, shattering sewers and water mains and spewing out hundreds of thousands of tonnes of sodden grey silt. And in the hill suburbs from Cashmere to Sumner there had been massive damage, not only from the shaking but from boulders that cascaded off the hills.

The city centre was a ruin. Almost all the Gothic stone buildings that characterised it had fallen, in whole or in part. A 26-storey hotel was leaning at a perilous angle and two modern buildings had simply collapsed on their occupants.

The area within the four avenues was cordoned off within hours. Civil Defence set up base in the Christchurch Art Gallery, a building that the layman would have expected to have been reduced to nothing more than shards of glass. The air became thick with the chunk of helicopters, many of them hired by the media.

Search and Rescue teams flew in from all over the world and were applauded at the airport. But there were none of the miracle survivals that the media feast on. The last live rescue happened on the day after the quake. Thereafter all those feared dead were dead. The highest toll was in the Canterbury Television building, which also housed a language school. It seemed particularly unfair that so many of the dead should be both young and foreign. It wasn't their quake.

Briefly Christchurch became one of those televisual disasters that we have all witnessed, when rapidly forgotten the media machine moves on from the disaster like Pac-Man in search of more drama to consume. And sure enough, within a few days we had dropped off the bottom of the international bulletins, to be replaced by a landslide in Bolivia.

The country's first ever national emergency was declared, which granted the authorities almost unlimited powers. People accepted a form of martial law. The new uniform of authority was a hard hat, a clipboard and a high-vis vest.

The CBD belonged to the authorities, but in the suburbs people set to work. An army of students, hundreds strong, marched into the east of the city and attacked the silt with shovels and barrows and strong young limbs. Farmers poured into town with front-end loaders. Money poured in from the rest of New Zealand. There were innumerable acts of selflessness and generosity. People praised the Canterbury spirit, the Kiwi resilience. It was understandable self-flattery. People just did what people everywhere do in a crisis. In some ways it was easier to be in the thick of it than to be far away. You were able to do something.

Mending power lines and water pipes is less glamorous work than search and rescue, but heroic things were achieved. Working round the clock, the lines company restored power to some within hours, to most in a week. Water took longer, and it will be months before there is a fully functioning sewerage system. But water tankers appeared quickly in suburban centres, and Portaloos on street corners, followed later by chemical toilets. People discovered how much of the day can be consumed in simply achieving the basics of food, water and shelter, but almost everyone accepted that this was how things had to be. There was discomfort but little overt discontent. And in the first couple of weeks there was almost no looting.

Thousands left the city. Not fleeing, most of them, just leaving, because their houses were

The first ever national emergency was declared, which granted the authorities almost unlimited powers. People accepted a form of martial law. The new uniform of authority was a hard hat, a clipboard and a high-vis vest.

Christchurch has been presented with a rare opportunity.
We have the chance to build a better city.

uninhabitable. At the time of writing, the official estimate is that 10,000 homes may have to be demolished. But no-one knows for sure. And no-one knows whether some suburbs will have to be abandoned in their entirety.

The cordon round the central city was absolute. Owners of vehicles were unable to collect them. Owners of businesses were unable to access stock or records. Some three weeks after the quake a few building owners stormed the barricades. They didn't get far, but they made their point. The emergency authorities acknowledged, grudgingly, that they could have communicated better. Bit by bit the cordon was lifted.

Only the eminent were allowed under the danger tape to gawp at the spireless cathedral, the fallen statues of Godley and Scott, the toppling Grand Chancellor Hotel. One of the eminent was Prince William, doing a rapid-fire tour of southern hemisphere disasters a month or so before his wedding.

Because of his visit a memorial service was hastily put together in Hagley Park. It seemed too early; there were still unidentified remains in the rubble. But a big crowd gathered in the autumn sunshine and the dignitaries said what needed to be said and the bishops said what the faithful wanted to hear and Dame Malvina Major sang a duet with a cathedral chorister and Hayley Westenra sang 'Amazing Grace' and Dave Dobbyn sang and the Crusaders anthem was played, and despite its oddity the service seemed to do the cathartic trick for those attending.

Ken Ring the Moon Man became infamous. He predicted another big quake and named a date. Though he had spectacularly failed to predict the two biggest earthquakes in the city's history, he nevertheless managed to worry many. What he appeared to offer was certainty in a world that had become uncertain and with terra firma no longer firma some people were willing to cling to even the appearance of knowledge. On the weekend of his prediction thousands left town and, sure enough, late that Sunday evening there was an aftershock measuring 5.1. Those who believed felt vindicated. Others pointed out that with aftershocks occurring daily, the Moon Man could hardly miss.

His predictions filled a gap normally occupied by science. For it had become clear that the geophysicists and seismologists were effectively as ignorant as the rest of us. They had not even known of the existence of the fault that broke the city, and they could tell us nothing for sure about the future.

The quake brought Christchurch face to face with a harsh and simple truth: we live on the cooling crust of a molten planet and it is utterly indifferent to our wellbeing. We are, in short, like ticks on a rhino.

We knew this already if we cared to think about it, but there is a vast difference between knowing a truth intellectually and being thrust up against it by experience.

At the time of writing, we are already into autumn and the weather has turned cool. It is going to be a long winter. A government department has been created to oversee the reconstruction of the city, but the task is so vast, the problems so various, that there is no sense yet of any way ahead.

The golfer I mentioned earlier told me that in the Chinese language the character representing the concept of disaster also represents the concept of opportunity. I don't know whether that's true, but it's apt. Christchurch has been presented with a rare opportunity. We have the chance to build a better city. There is no shortage of ideas on how to do it. Big, bold decisions will have to be made. But what is unclear at this stage is how they will be made. Will a single wise, broad-shouldered man or woman emerge to lead the recovery? Will the people be consulted and if so, how? Will we drown in the glue of bureaucracy? Nobody knows. Right now this is a city of uncertainty.

We'll know perhaps 10 years from now. If, then, you can stand in the heart of Christchurch, look around and say, 'Now that's how you rebuild a city', then we'll have passed a test of sorts. Meanwhile we live day to day (and as I type this sentence at 11.15am on 20 April 2011, an aftershock rattles the house and my dog has come running to the study in search of company and reassurance; he is not alone.).

On the day of the quake a friend drove to Brighton to rescue his elderly mother. The journey took him hours. Bridges were impassable, roads swamped with water and silt. But he collected his mum from amid a sea of silt 30cm or more deep and took her to the comparative peace of Lyttelton. A few days later he returned to fetch some things. Much had already happened. The streets were by and large cleared. And every last scrap of the silt that surrounded her house had gone, in its place a notice. 'Good luck,' it said, 'The Oxford Rugby Club.' It was almost worth having a quake for, he said.

EARTHQUAKE: A shaking, trembling or concussion of the earth due to subterranean causes often accompanied by a rumbling noise. The waves of shock sometimes traverse half a hemisphere destroying cities and many lives.

Webster's English Dictionary, 1906

The Calm Before ... ◆ ◆ ◆

Chris Moore

OPPOSITE: *The shining city — Christchurch as it was before the 22 February earthquake wrenched the heart from the city and the community.*

PHOTO: DAVID HALLETT

On 22 February 2011, Christchurch wakes to a cool, overcast dawn with a hint of rain. Across the city centre and through its suburbs 400,000 people are preparing for another weekday.

The main story in the morning's *Press* features a teacher's resignation following an alleged affair with a student. Elsewhere in the news, columnist Chris Trotter suggests a New Zealand cultural revolution against complacency, delusion and distractions. Air New Zealand announces plans to expand its air links with Japan, and delegates at a high-powered two-day New Zealand–United States forum

continue discussions on trade and world politics. While the debate continues in the correspondence columns about Christchurch mayor Bob Parker's recent controversial attendance at a symposium on earthquakes in Nepal, Christchurch plans to host the New Zealand Golf Open, with a possible injection of $20 million into a local economy still recovering from the 4 September 2010 earthquake.

There are other daily reminders of that event. Commuters travelling into the city's centre pass buildings mauled by the tremor and a severe aftershock on Boxing Day. Christchurch still carries the physical and

ABOVE: *The beating heart of the city — crowds in Cathedral Square watch the Topp Twins perform in the 2011 World Buskers Festival.*

PHOTO: CARYS MONTEATH

mental scars of these quakes. It has also learned to live with continuing tremors with a well-developed gallows humour. 'Keep calm and carry on' has become the city's unofficial rallying cry . . . or conversely, as one wit adds, 'Panic and freak out.'

'We laugh at anything less than a 4.1,' visitors alarmed by a passing 'wobble' are told.

By the summer of 2011, earthquakes have become an accepted, albeit uncomfortable, part of daily life in a community which once assumed, with a hint of smugness, that it was immune to seismic activity. Admittedly, an earthquake in 1888 had dislodged the top of the city's Anglican cathedral spire but the event had long passed into folk legend. Apart from the vicarious excitement of the occasional tremor, Christchurch appeared as solidly immovable as its fine nineteenth-century Gothic Revival buildings, comfortable rows of Victorian and Edwardian shop fronts and sleek, modern office blocks.

But the earthquake of 4 September and its aftermath has changed all this. The 7.1 tremor in the pre-dawn darkness of a

ABOVE RIGHT:

An exhibition at the Christchurch Art Gallery raised issues of development and regeneration following the 2010 earthquake.

PHOTO: DON SCOTT

cold Saturday morning caused serious and extensive structural damage. Liquefaction seemed to have melted the solid Canterbury earth. No lives were lost, but it was a sobering warning against complacency.

Five months later mangled brick walls, sagging timbers and no-go zones continue to bear witness to the power of the earthquake. But slowly, deliberately, Christchurch is picking itself up, dusting itself down and carrying on with business.

On 22 February the city's pulse beats steadily. By noon, the streets are filled with lunchtime crowds. Tourists and workers on a lunchbreak mingle with English language students on Colombo Street. Ballantynes,

that symbol of commercial Christchurch, is crowded with shoppers.

In *The Press*'s offices in the Square, final preparations are well in hand for the move from the landmark building the newspaper has occupied since 1909 to a new office block in Gloucester Street.

Across the Square in Christ Church Cathedral, visitors stand beneath its graceful Gothic arches to admire both the heritage architecture and colourful displays for the city's annual Festival of Flowers. The more energetic trudge up the narrow, twisting staircase to the spire's balcony for panoramic views of the city as the old Post Office clock strikes 12.30pm. Below them, coffee shop

ABOVE: *Five months after the September earthquake, life was slowly returning to normal in Christchurch. Shortly before 22 February, this was the scene in Colombo Street, Sydenham.*

PHOTO: DON SCOTT

tables in Cashel Street are rapidly filling.

To the city's southeast lies the historic port town of Lyttelton — Canterbury's gateway to the sea since the first European settlers arrived in 1850. Ground delicatessen and café is doing brisk business while the Volcano restaurant across the street is readying itself for the night's diners. Below, in the port, passengers board the Diamond Harbour ferry *Black Diamond* for the run across the harbour to the small seaside community on the fringe of Banks

Peninsula. Traffic flows along Norwich Quay and through the Lyttelton tunnel deep beneath the Port Hills.

It is now 12.45pm. Beneath the tunnel's northern portal, subterranean pressures are pushing against a fault zone 10km below the earth's surface, one of the complex web of fractures seismologists believe thread an ancient intricate path across the Canterbury Plains. The 4 September earthquake and Boxing Day aftershock have already revealed the potency of this skein of faults. But the earth has not yet finished with Christchurch.

At 12.51pm the fault beneath the tunnel can no longer resist the immense pressures. It ruptures, dispatching shockwaves upwards towards the oblivious city and through the Port Hills to the sea beyond. In the seconds which follow, the earth writhes and roars like a wounded animal, gripping Christchurch in a web of destruction.

This will be a day unlike any other.

ABOVE: *Many large buildings in central Christchurch were extensively damaged in the 2010 earthquake and its aftershocks. The Manchester Courts building at the intersection of Manchester and Hereford streets was among the casualties. Its demolition began in October 2010 and was completed at the end of January 2011.*

PHOTO: JOHN KIRK-ANDERSON

RIGHT: *Crews demolish shops in Colombo Street, Beckenham, in January 2011. The buildings were condemned after suffering major damage in the September 2010 earthquake.*

PHOTO: DAVID HALLETT

Destruction — Christchurch's Cathedral of the Blessed Sacrament was among the first casualties of the earthquake as its majestic façade, designed by Francis Petre and completed in 1905, broke apart and collapsed. PHOTO: KIRK HARGREAVES

. . . the Storm

Chris Moore

I am become Death, the shatterer of worlds. — Bhagavad Gita

ABOVE RIGHT: *The steel supports put in place after the September 2010 earthquake were virtually all that remained of the historic Durham Street Methodist Church after the February earthquake. Three men inside the building died. Built in 1865, the church was among many fine heritage buildings destroyed or severely damaged by the tremor.*

PHOTO: CARYS MONTEATH

The tremor struck Christchurch in a monstrous physical blow, 'as if you were punched by a heavyweight boxer', someone later remembered. It was followed by 20 seconds of violent shuddering; an eternity for those caught inside buildings or huddled outside on streets and in malls.

As the earth heaved and tossed, entire swathes of the city, especially older brick buildings, crumbled and fell. Bricks, concrete, glass and entire verandahs cascaded down onto Cashel Mall as pedestrians and shoppers scattered, scrambling for safe ground or any shelter, however fragile, which offered some protection. A young mother holding her baby in her arms ran outside only to be struck by falling debris. She was injured, but survived to be reunited with her child later. A pastry baker in the Trocadero Bakery, 42-year-old Shane Tomlin fell

with the building's floors as it collapsed. Severely injured, Tomlin was comforted by his rescuers. The man whose grime-covered face came to symbolise the horror of those traumatic minutes died later in hospital.

Lincoln University lecturer Ann Brower was on the No. 3 bus when it was crushed by falling rubble. Several people died, but Brower was eventually rescued, suffering a broken leg and severed tendons in her hand. Rope access technician Dennis Haskell held her hand as her rescuers struggled to release her.

'It's probably quite selfish — I should have let him talk to other people — but he stayed with me,' she said later.

Modern high-rise buildings appeared to sway and twist in a surreal dance as the tremor's violence shattered windows and sections of external walls. The Forsyth Barr building on the intersection of Colombo

ABOVE LEFT: *The devastation of the central city is shown in this image of Manchester Street from Gloucester Street.*
PHOTO: IAIN MCGREGOR

and Armagh streets appeared to bow outwards towards the street before swaying back, its reflective glass vibrating. Asphalt and concrete roads and pavements billowed, cracked or opened into deep fissures.

Close by in Colombo Street workers from nearby buildings fought to save trapped passengers from two buses crushed by rubble.

Inside Christ Church Cathedral staff and visitors huddled beneath doorways or arches desperately holding each other as the building lurched. As she crouched in a door frame, the cathedral's theologian in residence, the Reverend Lynda Patterson, listened for the familiar sound of the cathedral bells which had always rung in earlier major tremors. All she now heard was the rumble of falling masonry as the cathedral's elegant tower and spire, damaged by earlier earthquakes in 1881,

1888, 1901 and 1922, tottered and fell back, demolishing the western side of the nave.

One by one other heritage buildings fell victim to the earthquake. The majestic facade of the Catholic Cathedral of the Blessed Sacrament with its twin Italian Renaissance-style bell towers broke apart.

The stone chamber of the Provincial Council buildings — an opulent Victorian Gothic Revival hall filled with glowing paintings and dominated by a majestic vaulted ceiling — subsided into an amorphous pile of grey rubble. Watched by a passing busload of frightened school children, the Durham Street Methodist Church, Christchurch's first stone church, collapsed, killing three men who had been working inside to restore its organ.

Bars and restaurants along the city's popular Oxford Terrace and in the

ABOVE: *Manchester Street was filled with lunchtime crowds minutes before the earthquake. Shortly afterwards it lay in ruins, cars buried in rubble and rows of shops gutted by the tremor.*

PHOTO: CARYS MONTEATH

fashionable Sol Square and Poplar Lane areas disintegrated as lunchtime crowds and diners ran for their lives.

Inside the Iconic Bar at the corner of Manchester and Gloucester streets, Amy Cooney and her brother Jaime Gilbert had begun their working day in the popular inner-city bar. It was Gilbert's first day as the Iconic's senior barman.

As the shaking built to a crescendo Cooney looked at her brother and told him to get out of the building. She had reached the gutter when Gilbert called to her.

'I think he wanted to shield me. We only managed to get each other's hand when the rubble came down. I was knocked out, but when I came around I realised I still held my brother's hand.'

She called to him but the brother who had tried to protect her was dying.

'"Bro, bro are you all right?" I just kept calling for him . . . then I felt his grip release.'

The youngest person to die in the earthquake was five-month-old Baxtor Gowland. The oldest victim was 82-year-old Donald Cowley.

ABOVE: *An area was cordoned off after the front wall of a row of shops at Merivale Mall collapsed onto Papanui Road.*

PHOTO: REUTERS

a As the tremor continued, a viscous grey sludge bubbled to the earth's surface, creating a sinister tide of silt and water which flowed through streets and into suburban driveways. In places the liquefaction created deep craters which swallowed cars and vehicles. In Hagley Park, century-old oak trees toppled after their roots lost grip in the liquefying soil. The clear water of the Avon River became a grey polluted wastepipe.

On the second floor of *The Press*, music writer and columnist Vicki Anderson peered out from beneath her desk while the office, part of a relatively new structure extending out from the original building, seemed to gyrate. She was immediately struck by a piece of falling ceiling tile.

'I yelled an obscenity at the top of my lungs but it was drowned out by the sound of our building falling down around us. Across the room from under their desk someone was yelling "yahoo" like it was a fun ride.'

In Cathedral Square, Japanese tourist Shogo Osawa kept his video camera operating. What he recorded became one of the most vivid visual images of the earthquake. Buildings are shrouded in a thick red blanket of dust. The truncated cathedral tower looms through the swirling dust cloud like a decayed tooth. Rubble crushes the colourful flowers and topiary of the floral displays outside the cathedral's west door. Across the Square, the bronze statue of the city's nineteenth-century founding father, John Robert Godley, lies toppled from its pedestal, prone and undignified on the paving stones.

Osawa's video also traps shouts, screams and a small child's hysterical cries emerging from the chaos. A policeman strides across the Square urgently telling people to move away from buildings. Couples embrace each other. Osawa's own wavering voice is heard, 'The cathedral just fell. Oh God, it's unreal. Unreal.'

Inside Christ Church Cathedral, artist Sue Spigel was working in her studio — a small room up a flight of stairs off the nave. She had decided to go for a cup of tea, but, distracted by something on the radio, sat down in a window seat to listen. Moments later, the cathedral began falling apart.

Spigel attempted to get under a table. 'Within about four seconds, a huge piece of masonry fell on both tables, crushing them.

ABOVE: *Christ Church Cathedral artist Sue Spigel was trapped in her studio after the cathedral's spire collapsed into the nave. Despite suffering a broken arm and lacerations, she managed to open a window and call for help. Watched by hundreds of onlookers, Spigel was rescued and has recovered.*

PHOTO: RICHARD COSGROVE

ABOVE: *The horror —
passengers were trapped in
these two buses crushed by
falling masonry in Colombo
Street. Despite the valiant
attempts by passers-by to
rescue them, some died and
others were badly injured.*
PHOTO: REUTERS

If I had been under there or at my sewing
machine, I would have been dead,' she said.

As the world collapsed around her, the
window she desperately clung to became
her lifeline.

'I was up to my neck in rubble, but I was
able to push myself up onto the window sill
with one arm as my other arm was broken.
Then everything went black when the rest
of the tower fell and with all the dust and
dirt, it was like a tornado.'

When the dust cleared, and battling
the pain from her fractured arm, she leant

from the window to cry out for help. Below,
hundreds of people looked up at Spigel's
battered and bloodied figure. Eventually a
policeman pushed his way through. Assisted
by onlookers he helped her slowly climb
down a ladder before she was ferried in a
police-escorted station wagon to hospital.

The Dean of the cathedral, the Very
Reverend Peter Beck, rushed from his office
to stand outside, briefly traumatised by
the devastation surrounding him. He did
not know how many people were trapped,
possibly dead, in the wrecked cathedral. After

The vivid red of a kinetic sculpture
by artist Phil Price (lower right)
stands unscathed against the rubble
and destruction at the intersection of
Manchester, High and Lichfield streets.

PHOTO: DON SCOTT

a few moments, the popular and energetic clergyman recovered his composure.

'This is about people and lives,' he said, looking at the hundreds of individuals milling around him. 'We've got to take care of one another, pray for each other.'

Behind him *The Press* building's roof had collapsed sideways onto the third floor. Inside the paper's finance department and cafeteria, employees, some critically injured, lay pinned by layers of concrete and steel. One member of the newspaper's 'family', Adrienne Lindsay, was already dead. Unaware of the situation upstairs, colleagues on the floors below struggled to evacuate the building.

Away from the central business district, the earthquake's immediate effects were equally apocalyptic. In suburban streets from New Brighton to Fendalton, brickwork and tiled roofs disintegrated, roads fragmented.

At Aranui High School in the east, teacher Chris Henderson sheltered under a doorway, but the earthquake's force tossed him sideways. A power box narrowly missed his head as it fell from the wall. A pupil was knocked unconscious when the roof of the school's music block collapsed. Thankfully only 40 pupils were in the school after a PPTA union meeting had halted classes at lunchtime.

On the fifth floor of the Christchurch City Council offices, councillors and staff were thrown violently against walls and furniture as the shockwaves rolled across

the city. A cup of scalding tea spilled onto one councillor. Caught in the chaos, she was oblivious to the pain.

In Lyttelton, people dived for safety as entire rows of familiar buildings disintegrated. In the town's library, staff and customers cowered beneath tables as books, shelves and water from broken pipes cascaded down. Across the road, the exterior walls of Ground café and the nearby Volcano restaurant shook and crumpled. The Lyttelton Coffee Company had recently been earthquake-strengthened

ABOVE: *The Dean of Christ Church Cathedral, Peter Beck, appears overwhelmed by the level of destruction to the city's iconic church. 'We've got to take care of one another, pray for each other,' he said. Despite initial fears that up to 20 people might have been killed in the collapse of the tower, search teams found no bodies.*

PHOTO: RICHARD COSGROVE

The destruction of a
Christchurch symbol —
the ruined Christ Church
Cathedral.

PHOTO: JOHN KIRK-ANDERSON

LEFT: *The historic port town of Lyttelton lay near the earthquake's epicentre and was extensively damaged. This car was smothered by falling debris.*

PHOTO: NATASHA MARTIN

but this did not prevent its heavy verandah crashing down against the frontage.

On Norwich Quay, the port's original seafront, the earthquake demolished rows of buildings, including many of Lyttelton's landmark pubs. The earthquake did not discriminate along sectarian lines either — the town's Presbyterian, Catholic and Anglican churches were all severely damaged.

As it slipped away from the wharf, the 12.50pm Diamond Harbour ferry was suddenly caught in a washing machine as the sea threshed violently. Above it dust from the fallen buildings rose into the afternoon sky as buildings in Lyttelton's main street collapsed.

On the other side of the Port Hills, in the Christchurch Gondola complex, operator Michelle English saw — and heard — an avalanche of rocks and boulders crashing down the steep hillside above. She screamed at visitors to leave the glass-clad building, pushing some through the door seconds before the rocks crashed into the structure. Two terrified American tourists, trapped in a small swaying gondola cabin high above the hillside, were later rescued by staff.

St Albans, Sumner, Redcliffs, New Brighton and Sydenham were among the hardest-hit suburbs. As rows of shops collapsed in Sydenham, rocks crashed down on Sumner as huge slices of cliff were shaken to bits by the earthquake. Owners of expensive houses and modest seaside homes alike found themselves teetering on the edge of an abyss. The familiar Sumner landmark,

The 12.50pm Diamond Harbour ferry was suddenly caught in a washing machine as the sea threshed violently. Above it dust from the fallen buildings rose into the afternoon sky as buildings in Lyttelton's main street collapsed.

ABOVE: *Shattered buildings in Oxford Street near Lyttelton's commercial heart.*

PHOTO: KIRK HARGREAVES

Shag Rock, simply exploded into fragments.

Slowly the first tremor died away leaving streets full of dazed, shocked crowds and filled with acrid dust, fallen debris and the insistent banshee wail of sirens and alarms. People began to emerge from buildings, distressed, stunned, injured. But there was little or no panic as groups and individuals defied the chaos to comfort and reassure the traumatised, care for the injured or talk quietly among themselves. It was a time when strangers became friends and samaritans.

Other individuals helped police and firefighters to release the trapped from unstable wreckage and buildings. In the moments during and after the earthquake Christchurch saw many acts of quiet heroism.

Then came a major aftershock, followed closely by another, both accompanied by the familiar crack and crash of falling masonry and debris. There were shouts and cries as people knelt or sat on the vibrating ground,

29

Before 22 February, the old Canterbury Provincial Chambers was one of the jewels in Christchurch's architectural crown; a collection of fine nineteenth-century Gothic Revival buildings. The earthquake destroyed its centrepiece, the Provincial Council Chambers (right) and badly damaged other parts of the complex.

PHOTO: DON SCOTT

ABOVE: *Within minutes of the first tremor people began to assemble in the comparative safety of Cathedral Square. Surrounded by debris and rubble, they comforted and supported each other as aftershocks continued.*

PHOTO: RICHARD COSGROVE

looking up apprehensively at what had previously been reassuringly solid buildings. High above Victoria Square, office workers trapped in the Forsyth Barr building after the building's stairs collapsed, looked down as firefighters attempted to rescue them. Nearby there were reports of a gas leak.

As authorities warned of a heavy toll of dead and injured, hundreds of people of all ages and every background began to walk towards the open spaces of Hagley Park. Construction workers trudging alongside lawyers, mothers with children in prams being helped by school students, the elderly arm in arm with teenagers, all picking their way through the rubble and debris. Outside the collapsed Provincial Chambers in

Gloucester Street, a woman slumped to the ground, sobbing loudly. A man bent down, placed a comforting arm around her and helped her on.

Outside a hotel, a Japanese tourist insisted that he wanted to go in to recover belongings. Protesting loudly he was led away by other members of his party.

At Hagley Park, volunteer helpers struggled with heavy benches from the

LEFT: *An ambulance passes the broken remains of the Provincial Chambers complex in Armagh Street. The Christchurch ambulance service was overwhelmed by emergency calls in the hours following the tremor. Rescue teams from throughout the country soon began arriving in the city to assist emergency crews.*

PHOTO: RICHARD COSGROVE

neighbouring bowling club or erected tents to shelter the growing numbers of evacuees arriving at the gates. Medical teams — many delegates to a major medical conference in the city — formed an emergency triage team.

'Welcome to Hotel Hagley,' a cheerful young American emergency worker greeted new arrivals as the helicopters whirred overhead.

As it began to rain gently, Christchurch's long, anxious night of waiting had just begun.

Two hours after the tremor, Christchurch's central business district was cordoned off and people were evacuating the city. The camera catches the dust rising from wrecked buildings in Durham Street during a major aftershock.

PHOTO: STACY SQUIRES

IN CASHEL MALL

LEFT: *The faces of a disaster — Press reporter Olivia Carville comforts a badly injured Jane Taylor in Cashel Mall. Taylor suffered extensive injuries when the building she was in collapsed during the earthquake. Carville comforted her until medical teams arrived.*

PHOTO: JOHN KIRK-ANDERSON

Press **reporter Olivia Carville was out on Christchurch's streets immediately after the earthquake. She filed this report.**

The city of Christchurch looks like a war zone. Buildings are flattened, streets are violently ruptured and dead bodies lie in Cashel Mall covered with old towels and T-shirts.

Water and silt have swamped areas of the city, and smoke and dust blankets central Christchurch as dazed people wander through the streets in shock. Helicopters are flying overhead, carrying large water buckets to empty on smouldering buildings.

Bricks, glass and debris litter the streets and emergency services workers try desperately to rescue people trapped in the mountains of rubble. A backpacker's body lies in a van, crushed by a fallen building on Gloucester Street. A building on the corner of Lichfield and Manchester streets has been flattened and 30 emergency services workers sift through the rubble for bodies.

One woman's body has been dragged out of the destruction and lies on the side of the street covered in an old green towel as officials rush around her trying to save others. People in sneakers and bike helmets comb through the ruins trying to help. A young man watches as diggers drag huge pieces of debris away from the site; he believes his brother is underneath this crumpled building.

A seriously injured man fell through the floor of a shop in Cashel Mall during the quake and is carried out by six members of the public. One woman who worked in Cashel Mall has a broken pelvis and a severe gash exposing bone on her face, but an ambulance cannot reach her for more than an hour because emergency services are stretched to capacity.

I try to help her, holding her pelvis together. She is screaming in pain.

RIGHT: *Surrounded by the ruins of Cashel Mall in central Christchurch, Nathan Pilkington cradles his six-year-old daughter Nevada. Behind them rescue crews battle to reach people trapped in the rubble.*

PHOTO: IAIN MCGREGOR

Bricks, glass and debris litter the streets and emergency services workers try desperately to rescue people trapped in the mountains of rubble.

IN CASHEL MALL

Members of the public try to comfort her, and one man says, 'Put this on your face, try to hold your face together.' I leave when her husband arrives.

Emergency services workers have been pulled in from all areas of Canterbury to assist in the immediate search and recovery operation. Ambulance officers, firefighters and police direct dazed residents out of the CBD and set up temporary cordons around it.

People shocked, crying and injured gather in groups to support one another on the outskirts of the city. Cell phone contact and internet connections have been cut in the aftermath of the quake and distressed residents struggle to reach loved ones.

The city continues to heave and shake right throughout the day as those trapped in the central city flock to evacuation havens such as Latimer Square and Hagley Park.

The seriously injured lie on blankets in Latimer Square waiting for medical attention. St John Ambulance medics set up triage tents as more injured people keep arriving, some screaming as the aftershocks continue.

ABOVE: *Rescuers gently lift an injured woman from the ruins of a central-city building. Christchurch saw many acts of quiet bravery during the hours and days after the earthquake as people often risked their lives to help others.*

PHOTO: IAIN MCGREGOR

ABOVE LEFT: *People comfort each other outside a ruined building in Cashel Mall.*

PHOTO: JOHN KIRK-ANDERSON

ABOVE: *Good samaritans — A group of office workers make their way to safety in the central business district. This was a time when friends, colleagues and strangers gave support and help to those in need.*

PHOTO: CARYS MONTEATH

RIGHT: *Shocked, bewildered and disorientated, crowds leave Cashel Mall after the first tremor left devastation, death and injury in its wake.*

PHOTO: IAIN MCGREGOR

The city's open spaces and parks sheltered many people on 22 February. Here they gather in Latimer Square as smoke from the collapsed Canterbury Television building drifts through the trees.

PHOTO: JOHN KIRK-ANDERSON

LEFT: *Before the earthquake — originally built for the Christchurch Drainage Board in 1967, The Pyne Gould Corporation building on Cambridge Terrace was later extensively refurbished. At the time of the February earthquake it housed a variety of financial and professional companies.*
PHOTO: STACY SQUIRES

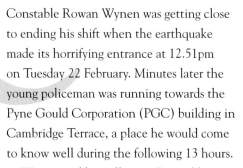

PGC and CTV

Chris Moore

Constable Rowan Wynen was getting close to ending his shift when the earthquake made its horrifying entrance at 12.51pm on Tuesday 22 February. Minutes later the young policeman was running towards the Pyne Gould Corporation (PGC) building in Cambridge Terrace, a place he would come to know well during the following 13 hours.

Wynen and his colleague Constable Peter Hansen were the first police officers

and emergency workers to reach the shattered building. Originally built in 1967 as offices for the Christchurch Drainage Board, the four-storey building was later redeveloped by the Pyne Gould Corporation. Designed around a central service core — a feature specifically designed to absorb the forces generated by an earthquake — the offices had sun shading, balconies and generous ceiling

ABOVE: *Minutes after he was rescued from the broken remains of the Pyne Gould Corporation building, Jeff McLay walks to safety after being trapped in the wreckage of what was his workplace.*

PHOTO: JOHN KIRK-ANDERSON

heights. On the day of the earthquake it housed a wide range of financial and professional firms whose staff enjoyed the pleasant views of the Edmonds Rotunda, a 1929 building designed in the Renaissance style with a graceful copper dome. Donated by local baking powder magnate Thomas Edmonds, the structure originally housed band concerts but had been converted into a restaurant.

Wynen's report of what followed the quake on 22 February still has a dreadful immediacy about it.

'The earthquake happened and it was about 30 seconds afterwards when the radios came back on and it was just mayhem,' he remembered.

Wynen and Hansen turned onto Manchester Street, where they first saw the PGC building. The building looked 'like

LEFT: *Constable Rowan Wynen was one of the first to arrive at the PGC building after the earthquake. He would work to rescue survivors from the wreckage for the next 13 hours. Here he waves onlookers back as aftershocks continue to strike the city.* PHOTO: YOUTUBE VIDEO FRAME GRAB

OPPOSITE: *Rescuers had to cut their way through layers of concrete and steel to reach people trapped in the PGC building.* PHOTO: JOHN KIRK-ANDERSON

PREVIOUS PAGES: *A day after the 22 February earthquake, rescue teams were continuing to comb the wrecked Pyne Gould Corporation Building for trapped survivors. The office block had become the focus of one of the city's most intense search, rescue and recovery operations. To the left of the building, the badly damaged Edmonds Rotunda still stands on the banks of the Avon River.* PHOTO: DON SCOTT

a pancake', reduced to two badly listing storeys of tangled and twisted concrete and metal. Inside dozens of workers were trapped, while many of their colleagues returning from lunch stood outside, distraught and disbelieving.

The minutes following the first tremor saw individual and collective heroism, as colleagues and passing strangers defied aftershocks to organise rescue parties and construct makeshift ladders and platforms to assist those who could still walk from the wrecked structure.

Wynen rushed around to the building's rear, and was joined minutes later by two firefighters.

'They ran from the central fire station with a ladder and we just made makeshift ladders out of whatever we had,' Wynen said.

'We climbed up to the first level. Once we were there, we found holes we could crawl into. It was amazing — people started crawling towards us once they could hear us. And we just pulled them down on the ladder or carried them out and walked them out.' Wynen helped 10 people from the building.

'We came up with a plan . . . the priority was those who were alive.' He also witnessed two amputations in the midst of the wreckage as medical teams struggled to save seriously injured victims.

'Two fire officers arrived not long after us and that was it for about two to three hours. Then the police started arriving and we were delegating jobs out, sending them away to get extraction tools. They had to raid places to get stuff. It was whatever we could grab at the time,' Wynen said.

'I spoke to three girls within the first three hours who were trapped in one corner of the

The building looked 'like a pancake', reduced to two badly listing storeys of tangled and twisted concrete and metal. Inside dozens of workers were trapped while many of their colleagues returning from lunch stood outside, distraught and disbelieving.

LEFT: *Free! The relief of being rescued is clearly seen on a woman's face as an emergency team help her down from the shattered building.*

PHOTO: JOHN KIRK-ANDERSON

OPPOSITE: *The extent of damage to the PGC building can be seen in this photograph taken from street level. The orange marks indicate the different floors of the building.*

PHOTO: DON SCOTT

building. I went underneath the building and I could talk to them through the concrete. Seeing them come out several hours later was probably the highlight of it all. Not being able to help them initially but seeing them walk out several hours later was great.'

More emergency workers arrived at the site as the PGC building became the focus of one of the most concentrated rescue attempts in Christchurch during the first days after the quake. About 3am on Thursday, Rowan Wynen finally went home, desperate for rest and to see his partner.

Rescue efforts continued around the clock at the site for several days, until it was clear no further survivors would be recovered.

ABOVE: An office worker is led gently down to safety from one of the upper levels of the PGC building.

PHOTO: JOHN KIRK-ANDERSON

LEFT: After many anxious minutes, this office worker from the PGC building was lowered down from her shaky perch in a hoist manned by fire brigade and emergency personnel.

PHOTO: JOHN KIRK-ANDERSON

SMITH

CRANE & CONSTRUCTION LTD

RIGHT: *Helen Guiney was trapped in the PGC building for more than 20 hours before being located and rescued. It was a brief moment of celebration in a place where many people died or were seriously injured after the office block collapsed in the earthquake.*

PHOTO: DEREK FLYNN

LEFT: *As rescue teams struggled to reach those trapped in the PGC building following the 22 February tremor, their friends, colleagues and the public comforted and cared for the injured on the street below.*

PHOTO: RICHARD COSGROVE

LEFT: *What had once been a modern office block was reduced to a contorted mound of broken concrete and steel. Emergency teams continued working at the PGC building for several days but the search and rescue operation eventually became a search and recovery as hope faded for those still trapped.*

PHOTO: DON SCOTT

RIGHT: *David Sandeman (left) and Jeff McLay are ecstatic after being rescued from the PGC building by emergency workers.*

PHOTO: JOHN KIRK-ANDERSON

ABOVE: *Safely outside the PGC building, this group comforted each other while trying to make contact with family and friends. Scenes like this were repeated throughout the city in the hours after the earthquake.*

PHOTO: RICHARD COSGROVE

THE LAST SURVIVOR

LEFT: *The face of a survivor — Ann Bodkin was rescued from the PGC building with minor injuries after the building collapsed during the 22 February earthquake.*
PHOTO: STACY SQUIRES

Ann Bodkin, who spent 25 lonely hours entombed in the rubble of the PGC building after the 22 February earthquake, can credit the sharp senses of a television crew for her survival.

The rescue of the Education Review Office employee from the collapsed building on Cambridge Terrace was sparked by two members of the Australian media, who heard her cries for help from her 'concrete coffin', buried under tonnes of debris.

The Channel Nine television crew from Sydney — reporter Simon Bouda and cameraman Shaun Wellfare — were at the PGC building the day after the quake when Bouda thought he heard an unusual noise from the rubble. The pair were at the building following a New South Wales urban search and rescue team about to start a new shift at the site at about 11am.

'A fire engine was turned off and I heard a voice — a woman's voice,' Bouda said.

Wellfare thought the reporter was hearing things until he too heard a noise — a tapping from within the ruins. Immediately, the pair raced to tell firefighters there was someone else trapped and alive.

Silence fell across the site. Someone called out and Bodkin responded.

After her release from Christchurch Hospital, with only a sore shoulder and some

LEFT: *Search and rescue personnel establish contact with Ann Bodkin 25 hours after she was trapped in the collapse of the PGC building. She survived her ordeal with a sore shoulder and bruising.* PHOTO: ROBYN EDIE

THE LAST SURVIVOR

LEFT: *Cameraman Shaun Welfare (left) and reporter Simon Bouda of Sydney's Channel Nine were the first to hear Ann Bodkin's cry for help as they filmed a New South Wales urban search and rescue team at the PGC building.* PHOTO: STACY SQUIRES

BELOW: *Graham Richardson's face expressed it all after his wife, Ann Bodkin, was rescued from the PGC building.*

PHOTO: ROBYN EDIE

bruising to show for her ordeal, Bodkin spoke of her astonishing survival.

Pinned underneath the caved-in building and lying flat on her back, Bodkin became locked in a fight between fear and a dogged drive to get out. The 53-year-old was entombed about 20m inside the building.

Bodkin later said she would never forget the noise and violence of the earthquake as it 'pulled the building to bits'.

Bodkin was in her office on the third floor. 'I got up and hid under my desk — it was the safest place to be.' She had no sense she was falling, but as the building buckled, she was hit on the head by a ceiling panel and then another object. This second blow to Bodkin's shoulder could have been what saved her, because it pushed her onto her back as her surroundings closed in.

Following the building's collapse, she lay in a silent vault with just a speck of daylight shining through a small gap. Bodkin said there was debris about 10cm from her nose. She kept her limbs moving by propping herself up on her elbows, trying to stay mobile.

'I started calling out to see if there was anyone else around. But I was pretty much in a concrete coffin and no one could have heard me.' Bodkin drew on television footage she had seen of people being rescued days after a building collapse and steeled herself for a long wait. 'I thought, I have air and room; I can survive this. I pushed negative thoughts away and was determined to get out.'

A fire engine arrived almost straight after the building collapsed and she could hear workers freeing other people. Bodkin kept calling out, but the noise of the rescue effort drowned out her cries.

ABOVE: *An emergency worker reassures Ann Bodkin as she is carried from the PGC building following her rescue.*

PHOTO: CHRIS SKELTON

'And the problem for me was, every time they started drilling, the [fire] sprinklers started going.' She was still stuck, soaked and cold, when night fell, but there was some light from the rescuers outside.

During these dark hours, there were moments when her determination was broken by pangs of fear and Bodkin thought she might never get out. 'It happened only three or four times, but I had to keep pushing them [the negative thoughts] away.' It was the 'happiest moment' of her life when there was a break in the clamour, and she yelled out and finally received a response. Her determination and belief that she would be rescued was paying off, she said.

Search teams began talking to her and updating her on their progress as they inched through the twisted wreck, until a hand appeared through an opening.

Bodkin's extraction from the ruins — feet first and strapped to the end of a fire engine's ladder — into a waiting crowd of people, was not glamorous, but it was a triumph of resilience. 'I knew I would get out. But I also know I'm a very lucky girl.'

RIGHT: *The former NOW TV and Canterbury on Air Studios became the base for Canterbury Television. The six-storey building on the corner of Madras and Cashel streets also housed a medical centre, a nursing school, the Kings Education English School and counselling services. Its collapse claimed more than 100 lives.*

PHOTO: LIZ MCDONALD

Across the battered and bleeding city in Madras Street, horrified onlookers caught in the first tremor had watched as the facade of the seven-storey Canterbury Television building peeled off like a sardine can being opened by an invisible hand to reveal the building's inner structure, open to the world like a surreal doll's house. Worse followed. For a few brief seconds it appeared that the structure would survive but then slowly,

irrevocably, it too collapsed. The floors pancaked downwards in a cloud of acrid dust and spewed out metal, glass, furniture, files, paper, pens, dust and — worst of all for those who witnessed it — human bodies.

After the smothering blanket of dust lifted, the wrecked building caught fire with an intensity which shocked the first firefighters and police to arrive on the scene. Many of the dead simply evaporated in the all-consuming

ABOVE: *In the minutes following the collapse of the Canterbury Television building on 22 February, police, emergency workers and members of the public attempted to reach those trapped in the rubble. Their efforts were hampered when a fierce fire broke out.*

PHOTO: CARYS MONTEATH

heat. There were survivors and miracles from the holocaust but they were few.

Nilgun Kulpe was in a meeting with nine colleagues who worked at Relationship Services on the fifth floor of the building. 'We dropped like we were in an elevator. The noise was huge. Everything smashing, cracking, falling,' she said later.

Terrified and disorientated, the group clung together as they plummeted downwards.

Then everything stopped. The group's exit was blocked but, looking up, they saw a glimpse of daylight. The roof was open.

'I knew then we were safe. I looked out and saw we were only a few metres from the ground. It was a total miracle. When I looked at the building I wondered how anybody could have survived,' Kulpe said.

She and her companions survived, although three were seriously injured.

RIGHT: *Police and members of the public, including construction workers, are the first rescuers on the scene at the Canterbury Television building.*
PHOTO: CARYS MONTEATH

BELOW LEFT: *Clemency Mutze was in the Canterbury Television building when the earthquake struck. Injured, she managed to reach safety.*
PHOTO: CARYS MONTEATH

BELOW RIGHT: *Rescue workers remove a body from the collapsed Canterbury Television building.*
PHOTO: JOHN KIRK-ANDERSON

A wall containing the Canterbury Television building's lift shaft became a grim symbol of the destruction caused by the 22 February earthquake.

PHOTO: CARYS MONTEATH

ABOVE: A day before, this was a busy workplace and office. In a handful of seconds, the Canterbury Television building was reduced to a shapeless mound of broken concrete and tangled steel.

PHOTO: PHIL REID

LEFT: Firefighters dampen down the blackened remains of the Canterbury Television building after a major fire erupted following its collapse.

PHOTO: BLAIR ENSOR

ABOVE: *Darkness and aftershocks did not halt the rescue operation at the site of the Canterbury Television building as emergency workers fought to save those trapped in the wrecked building.*

PHOTO: JOHN KIRK-ANDERSON

Of the 13 people on the fifth floor, one woman died. Among the survivors was a boy who was waiting to see a counsellor for trauma resulting from the 4 September earthquake.

A part-time Canterbury University student, Quin Tang, was also working at Relationship Services on the fifth floor.

'When I was at a meeting in the building, I checked my watch at 12.50pm and thought, 10 minutes to go for my next appointment. Then the quake happened. The next time I checked my watch it was 2.30pm, when I decided to leave Latimer Square for home,' Tang said.

'In my memory, I was stepping out of the rubble hearing someone screaming "fire".'

She was rescued from the collapsed building by construction workers moments before the fire took hold.

'My first thought was wondering where my children were and if they were all right,' she said.

'A kind stranger gave me a lift part of the way home and I walked the rest of the way and was amazed to see that my house was standing and that my children were fine. It was only when I turned on the television that I realised the scale of what had happened to the building that I had

LEFT: *'It was a war zone. Chaos.'* Canterbury Police District Commander Dave Cliff reflects on his experiences during the Christchurch earthquake.

PHOTO: ROBERT KITCHIN

been working in.'

Tang's master's thesis had been due on 23 February but even after her ordeal, she still managed to submit it by 15 March.

'When it came to possessions in my house I thought that I could afford to lose anything else but not this piece of work,' Tang said. 'Now I know that it is in a safe place I feel that such a weight has been lifted. I'm not in a hurry to get the results. My part's done.'

Canterbury's senior police officer, Superintendent Dave Cliff, was among those co-ordinating the recovery effort, and also overseeing the exhaustive victim-identification process, including the 116 dead from the Canterbury Television building and the 94 dead in the PGC building.

On Tuesday 22 February, Cliff, a Napier man with 28 years' service in the police force, was in Wellington with Christchurch fire service manager Dan Coward and St John Ambulance South Island boss Chris Haines. The trio had flown up from Christchurch to speak at an emergency-management conference about dealing with natural disasters.

After the quake, and with the phone network down, Cliff was unable to get in touch with anyone in Christchurch. This forced the trio to arrange a helicopter to the city. On arrival, the helicopter circled the city to allow the three men to see the scale of the damage.

'There were hundreds of people sitting in the middle of Hagley Park and you could just see flooding, liquefaction and devastation everywhere.

RIGHT: *Rescue teams probe the wreckage of the Canterbury Television building's lift-well as work continued for several weeks on the site of the destroyed office block.*

PHOTO: CARYS MONTEATH

'There was a sense of disbelief. I think one of the sobering things was Dan Coward . . . Dan had a text from his wife saying basically "I need your help" but he couldn't get hold of her.'

Cliff said that on the day police had no idea how bad it was going to be. 'We knew there would be tens of people dead, but hundreds? No. You have to have an educated guess.'

Cliff said the city centre was a scene of chaos when he arrived, as rescue workers scrambled to save whoever they could from the ruins. 'Shortly after I arrived I went to the CTV site and there were literally hundreds of people working on that site, pulling away rubble and still rescuing people. I've never seen anything like it,' Cliff said.

He also spoke a little of what his own staff saw. 'There's a multitude of stories. One of our constables was assisting a surgeon in looking after a chap while he amputated his legs. I mean, to go through that. Another one of our staff who was out on the beat was running around with a couple of surgeons, who were triaging patients, saying "No, leave this person, this person can't survive. Move on to this one, they can be helped. This person requires an amputation." I wasn't there for that but the description . . . it sounded like a war zone. It was chaos.'

In the days which followed, the list of dead from both the Canterbury Television and PGC buildings increased. Jo Giles was a CTV host and a mother of four who represented New Zealand in pistol shooting

at two Oceania Games and a World Cup. She was one of New Zealand's first female jockeys and competed in motorsport and rock 'n' roll competitions.

Donna Merrie Manning, of Christchurch, was a CTV producer and presenter. Her former husband, Jonathan Manning, and their two children Kent and Lizzy, kept vigil outside the collapsed Canterbury Television building in the days after the quake.

Nina Jane Bishop, a Relationship Services administrator, had been a valued member of the administration team for 10 years. Chief executive Jeff Sanders remembered her as a woman with 'an amazing capacity for giving and caring for those around her, from friends to family and workmates'.

Trish Stephenson was a practice nurse

ABOVE: *The face of the missing — Hiroko Tamano was a student at the Kings Education English School in the Canterbury Television building. Her photo is a poignant reminder of the many young overseas students caught up in the destruction.*

PHOTO: DEREK FLYNN

ABOVE: *Urban search and rescue teams from New Zealand and China joined forces at the Canterbury Television building. More than 100 people died when it collapsed on 22 February, including 68 overseas students and nine teachers at the Kings Education English School.*

PHOTO: PHIL REID

who had relocated to the Canterbury Television building with medical practice The Clinic after damage to its Gloucester Street premises in the 4 September quake. A social, adventurous woman, she had booked a trip to Europe in May to visit family and retrace her father's footsteps as a soldier in World War II.

Haruki Hyakuman, of Japan, was studying English and hoped to become a nurse.

Yasuhiro Kitagawa, also of Japan, had arranged his study programme in Christchurch independently.

Phimphorn Liangchuea, of Thailand,

had two teenage children.

In the PGC building, the victims named included hockey player Amanda Hooper, who was working on the second floor. Hooper, 30, worked for Marac and had played for the Black Sticks in 2003.

There was also Blair James O'Connor, 34, of Christchurch, father of Caleb and Charlotte, an Oamaru man educated at St Kevin's College and Otago University. He had worked for Deloittes for two years and as a chartered accountant for Perpetual from 2004. Perpetual's Christchurch office was on the first floor of the PGC building.

The cleared Canterbury Television building site is a vivid reminder of the disaster's effect on the central city.
PHOTO: DON SCOTT

Flowers and tributes stand outside the site of the Canterbury Television building. The loss of life at this single location made it the focus for an outpouring of grief.

PHOTO: BARRY HARCOURT

RIGHT: *A family's vigil — Kent (left) and Lizzy Manning (right) and their father Jonathan spent the long hours in Latimer Square as they watched the rescue attempts at the Canterbury Television building and waited for news of their mother and former wife, CTV producer Donna Manning. Grief swept over the family, supported by friends and family, when police announced the rescue effort was being halted and would shift to a recovery operation.*
PHOTO: JASON SOUTH

At the site of the Canterbury Television building piles of rubble and a tall, skinny lift shaft, charred black by fire but not yet safe to take down, became a bleak memorial amid a yawning hole in the middle of the city.

Soon little remained of the places where scores of victims died. At the site of the Canterbury Television building, piles of rubble and a tall, skinny lift shaft, charred black by fire but not yet safe to take down, became a bleak memorial amid a yawning hole in the middle of the city. At one corner people left flowers on the waist-high orange plastic fencing encircling the site.

For Christchurch's mayor Bob Parker this site, more than any other, enshrined the full impact of the tragedy.

'In this building were people from all around the world. Young students here as guests in our city studying English. There were other small businesses that reached out to different people. They were here doing what they did every day.'

CTV RESCUER

Firefighter Paul Rodwell wriggled through a burning building, rattling with constant aftershocks, in a crawl space crammed with bodies and crushed furniture to save the lives of people he had never met.

Senior station officer Rodwell's efforts, and those of other rescue personnel, saw more than 20 people hauled alive from the wreckage that was once the PGC and Canterbury Television buildings.

Rodwell said the floor of the Canterbury Television building which housed the Kings Education language school, once 2.4m from floor to ceiling, had collapsed to little more than half a metre of space, crammed with rubble.

'Once you get inside there, in that tight space, aftershocks are coming and then the poisonous smoke is coming in there as well and you can't help thinking what it is like for those victims. At least I can wriggle out.

'Add to that [they] can't speak the language. They had smatterings of English which they were crying out from the dark — words like "dangerous", "serious".'

Rodwell said he saw two people still in their chairs, crushed into the foetal position and trapped by their legs. Fingers and toes were all that could be seen of other victims. A single concrete beam had trapped three students by their legs.

Unable to pronounce the names of the foreign students, he gave them nicknames, including one young man who he called Ken, whose leg had to be amputated.

ABOVE: *Senior station officer Paul Rodwell was among the emergency workers who struggled through rubble, noxious smoke and aftershocks to rescue survivors from the Canterbury Television building. He and his fellow team members saw more than 20 individuals hauled alive from the devastation.*

PHOTO: CHRIS SKELTON

Rodwell was forced to leave Ken alone with an oxygen mask, torch and pillow for two hours as search and rescue personnel dug down to him.

Being in the dark with the victims, giving them names and holding their hands made it personal, he said. 'Some people shut it out ... I like to empathise with them and when you're stuck down deep with them, you are with them, you know exactly how they feel although you can get out.'

It was a 'euphoric' feeling to get people out alive, he said. 'You actually feel privileged to be in a position where you have saved people. When you get into that position where you've saved four or five people, it's fantastic and I'm going to live my life knowing that.' He would like to meet the people he saved one day.

ABOVE: *Rescue teams confronted the confusion of rubble and debris in their search for the injured, trapped and, eventually, dead in the collapsed Canterbury Television building. They worked for days, carefully picking their way through the ruined office block metre by metre.* PHOTO: PHIL REID

FORSYTH BARR BUILDING

PHOTO: REUTERS

LEFT: *Preparation begins for the rescue descent of the office workers from the Forsyth Barr building.*

John Haynes doesn't think he's a hero. Haynes was among 15 people stuck on the sixth storey of the Forsyth Barr building at the corner of Armagh and Colombo streets on 22 February.

'We put it to them: There was a way out. If they wanted to come they could. If they wanted to stay they could stay,' Haynes said. The way out involved being lowered about 20m by a rope onto a car park, through which the trapped people could escape onto the streets.

'The building was going sideways, rocking, and then the stairs collapsed from the top to the bottom leaving no obvious means of getting out,' Haynes said. 'The guts of the building fell down 17 storeys. We just had a shell of a building.'

When the quake hit, smoke and dust rushed through the Forsyth Barr building leaving the 15 people trapped on the sixth floor. 'We met and the question was what do we do? In my mind there was a danger the building could collapse. The other was of fire.' Haynes said they could have remained 'stuck there but nobody would know if we were okay or not. It became obvious we needed to get out,' he said.

Haynes, a trained mountain guide who works as an investigator for the Office of the Ombudsmen, said he knew how to get the people down. After 9/11, office staff installed emergency supplies including rope, sledge hammers, axes and food in their Christchurch offices.

The trapped workers smashed a window and began preparing to descend the side of the building to safety. Uncertain about the strength of the ropes, a man 'of medium size' was sent down first. The rope held, and together with lawyer Grant Cameron, Haynes belayed 15 people down three and a half floors to the top of the car park where they

could walk down to the ground floor and escape.

Only Haynes and two others were left at the end. 'I said I'd get myself down last because I knew how to do that,' Haynes said.

He didn't have to. Fortunately he was rescued by a passing crane. 'I don't think I'm a hero. It was fortunate that I was able to do what I do. They were a fantastic bunch, no histrionics. They were willing to face the fact that it was a life or death situation.'

Assistant Ombudsman Christopher Littlewood, who was among those trapped, said, 'He [John] is a hero, that guy. John is a cool and calm fellow with huge experience in mountaineering. He's a person who rescued people from mountainsides. I knew I could trust him.'

Keith Lynch

ABOVE: *An office worker is slowly lowered down the Forsyth Barr building during the dramatic rescue of people trapped in the high-rise building during the quake. Other groups of people wait at broken windows to be rescued.*

PHOTO: JOHN KIRK-ANDERSON

An Unfortunate

Series of Events

Paul Gorman

LEFT: *Living above a ticking bomb — many Cantabrians were oblivious to the net of fault lines lying beneath the plains and the city.*

PHOTO: STACY SQUIRES

RIGHT: *In 1888, an earthquake toppled the top 7.8m of the Christ Church Cathedral's stone spire. Another tremor in 1901 broke off 1.5m. On 22 February 2011, spire and tower were demolished and the church severely damaged.*

PHOTO: ALEXANDER TURNBULL LIBRARY

Out of sight, out of mind. Such folly, as we all know now, when it comes to nature. Many Cantabrians probably thought a major earthquake would not happen in their lifetime, despite occasional warnings from scientists, council planners, engineers and Civil Defence workers that there was a good chance it would.

To those who paid attention to such alerts, the threat was thought most likely to come from the Alpine Fault, that slumbering giant of a gash in the landscape that courses along the western spine of the Southern Alps. The Hope Fault in North Canterbury was another suspect — a fault with form lying not too far away from the region's major population centre of Christchurch and which had brought down the spire of Christ Church Cathedral and caused extensive damage to the city in 1888.

Instead, it was hidden, or 'blind', faults under the Canterbury Plains that brought home to Cantabrians the fact that the ground beneath their feet was as unstable as that under many other parts of New Zealand. What happened on Saturday 4

RIGHT: *The Waimakariri River is one of the major forces in shaping and extending the Canterbury Plains.*

PHOTO: DON SCOTT

September 2010, at 4.35am and 42 seconds, and continued on Tuesday 22 February 2011, at 12.51pm and 42 seconds, proved in damaging, and then devastating and deadly, fashion that the enemy is closer than was thought.

Canterbury's fertile plains are the result of millions of years of mountain-building, then glaciation and river action washing away the eroded sediments. Vast fans of gravel, sand and silt have piled up around the Waimakariri and Rakaia rivers on top of basement rocks, slowly extending the plains eastwards and tying them to the volcanic rocks of Banks Peninsula.

As these deposits accumulated to become more than 500m thick in places, they masked the greywacke bedrock and the tell-tale splinters and cracks within that show faulting occurring under immense and relentless pressure from the colliding Pacific and Australian crustal plates.

The thick layer concealing what could be dozens of faults under the plains meant scientists did not know of the existence of the recently revealed Greendale Fault, and of the other faults that appear to have triggered its rupture on 4 September, nor of those leading to the 22 February quake. There was nothing in the landscape to

ABOVE: *Banks Peninsula's volcanic rocks are closely linked to the geology of the plains.*

PHOTO: DON SCOTT

suggest an active fault running from near Hororata to Rolleston, which meant it was not possible to determine how long ago it last ruptured, nor how long it was since the accompanying faults involved in the September quake last broke. GNS Science now believes it is at least 16,000 years since that happened, given that is when the river terraces at the end of the last glaciation were deposited and masked the faults.

It is even more difficult to put an approximate date on when the Port Hills Fault responsible for February's quake last broke. As well as being hidden under hundreds of metres of gravel, it is also buried under the Port Hills. It does not appear to break the surface, which makes it almost impossible for scientists to date. It may even be the first time it has ruptured in 100 million years.

Experts agree the September and February events were highly complex and some think such a sequence of events is very unlikely to happen again for thousands of years. In fact, they say the amount of stress released along the Port Hills Fault could take another 10,000 years to build up again before the next major event.

The river gravels have hidden Canterbury's earthquake secrets very well indeed. But the cat is now out of the bag.

It's not as if Canterbury geologists haven't warned for many years of the risks from hidden faults below the plains. Academic papers, doctoral theses and Civil Defence briefing papers all talk about the concealed threat for those interested enough to take notice of such matters. But it seems the potential menace was either not well communicated to much of the general public or perhaps not comprehended by them. Mention the Alpine Fault, though, and the chance of the 'Big One', and there is much greater recognition of what that might bring.

Scientists' descriptions of what lies beneath the gravels give some idea of how seismologically active Canterbury really is. GNS Science's Dr Kelvin Berryman has talked about the basement rocks 'looking like broken glass from millions of years of earthquake activity'. Retired Canterbury University structural geologist and active tectonics specialist Jocelyn Campbell, one of the gurus of faulting in the region, says there is a veritable 'spaghetti junction' of faults below the plains and in the Canterbury foothills.

ABOVE: *Deceptive calm — a skein of fault lines lies deep beneath the pastureland and river flats of the Canterbury Plains. This is the Rakaia River as it flows towards the sea.*

PHOTO: PETER MEECHAM

Scientists' descriptions of what lies beneath the gravels give some idea of how seismologically active Canterbury really is. GNS Science's Dr Kelvin Berryman has talked about the basement rocks 'looking like broken glass from millions of years of earthquake activity'.

More faults are also forming under the river gravels as the bedrock of the Chatham Rise off the Canterbury coast is forced back into the Southern Alps by the movement of the Pacific Plate.

'We've known for quite a long time that there are stirrings under a placid surface,' Campbell says. She says what has happened in Christchurch and Canterbury since September 2010 is evidence of that. It's the latest event in a pattern of faulting that has been repeated several times across the region over thousands of years and which is steadily moving southwards.

As blind faults below the plains start to crack and move up towards the surface, they lift the layers of sediment above into small, rolling hills called anticlines. The strength of the greywacke basement rocks means it takes a lot more energy to break the faults running through them than it does in softer rocks. As a consequence the greywackes have absorbed more strain before they finally rupture, and therefore generate large quakes.

Once triggered, several intersecting faults often split at much the same time and in a complicated way because of the development of these anticlines, forming a characteristic pattern that looks like short stitches placed across a long wound. That was the outcome of the 4 September event. Similar, older, structures exist in North Canterbury near Boby's Creek close to Mount Grey, also around Cust, and more recently further inland in the high country near the centre of the Arthur's Pass quake on 18 June 1994. Campbell says it is only a matter of geological time before another comparable fault structure crops up through the plains to the south of the Greendale Fault.

The June 1994 tremor gave Cantabrians an early warning of their vulnerability to big quakes from previously unrecognised faults. At 3.25pm on a sunny midwinter Saturday, an unknown fault ruptured at a depth of 4.3km about 10km southwest of Arthur's Pass generating a magnitude 6.7 quake. In a matter of seconds, seismic waves were rolling across the plains and into Christchurch, where buildings swayed, causing minor damage and widespread alarm. The quake was felt strongly in

Arthur's Pass township where damage was more widespread. State Highway 73 through the Otira Gorge was blocked by a large rockslide that partially dammed the Otira River, and two men in a truck had a narrow escape when two huge boulders missed their vehicle by only metres. The highway was closed because of cracks and rock falls elsewhere.

The quake, the largest on land in New Zealand at the time since the 1968 Inangahua earthquake, was followed by eight aftershocks of more than magnitude 5, with the largest a 6.1 shake about 36 hours later. The fault responsible did not break the surface, where the observed maximum movement was around 50cm.

Campbell points out on a series of maps how the cloud of aftershocks from that event slowly, over the years, has drifted roughly southwards from around the Harper River across Lake Coleridge and down the Rakaia River before squeezing out eastwards in much diluted form around the Malvern Hills towards Hororata. The possible implication is clear as the western end of the Greendale Fault lies not too far away. Did the big 1994 quake kick off a chain of events that led slowly but surely to what happened on 4 September 2010?

Whether or not that is actually the case, the theory illustrates how interconnected the faults, and the strain across them, are throughout Canterbury.

Campbell says many of the buried faults are 'basically all pointing at one place — Christchurch. It was always a matter of if, not when, these would start to arrive in our neck of the woods.'

Friday 3 September 2010 was a bleak, cold, early spring day in Canterbury. A biting southerly wind set in during the afternoon to batter the first daffodils of the season during the afternoon, accompanied by blustery rain and hail showers. Temperatures plummeted to

The cold night air slumbered peacefully and a thin sliver of moon began to rise in the cloudless skies shortly before 4am. Such tranquillity belied what was happening about 11km under the ground.

ABOVE: *The 4 September 2010 earthquake and its aftershocks were a traumatic wake-up call; a reminder of the threat that powerful earthquakes posed to a contemporary New Zealand city.* PHOTO: DAVID HALLETT

around 4 degrees Celsius. Further south, snow settled to close to sea-level; in Canterbury it lay down to a more respectable 300m on the hills. As night fell, the skies cleared, the wind dropped, and Cantabrians put on their spare duvets as frost began to form.

The cold night air slumbered peacefully and a thin sliver of moon began to rise in the cloudless skies shortly before 4am. Such tranquillity belied what was happening about 11km under the ground and 40km west of Christchurch, close to the quaintly named Charing Cross southeast of Darfield.

There, more than 16,000 years of unrelenting and escalating pressure had reached intolerable levels and events were rapidly building to a climax. The basement rocks had accommodated as much strain as they could. A network of faults was primed and ready to go.

Nobody will ever know exactly why it happened when it did. It could have held

off for the equivalent of a few more minutes in geological time, which might have amounted to several hundred more 'human' years. Instead, at 4.35am, the ground rose up and shook itself in rage.

For another hour or so, the waning moon continued to shine brightly, almost cruelly, down on a pitch-black Canterbury until dawn broke just after 6am across a shocked and frozen region. What had happened seemed surreal on that beautiful cloudless Christchurch spring morning, as the sun came up and lawns and roofs glittered cheerfully with frost.

The precise order of things is hard to determine. But it seems certain the magnitude 7.1 earthquake felt across nearly the whole country, that caused heavy damage throughout central Canterbury and Christchurch, and that defined the dawn of a new era for the region, was a concatenation of quakes. Everything that has happened seismologically since, including the deadly 22 February quake, is a result of the 30 to 40 seconds of chaos unleashed in the pre-dawn hours of that September morning.

Some people say they woke up just before the big quake hit but have no idea why. They may have felt a foreshock just a second or so ahead of the main event. Scientists believe the 7.1 shake was actually a consequence of at least three separate quakes occurring hot on the heels of each other, as three and possibly more faults broke almost simultaneously. The result

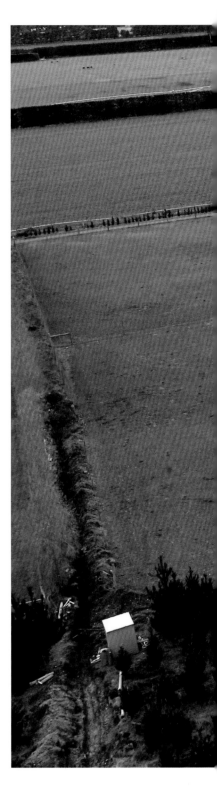

was a mix of seismic signals that have been difficult to interpret and tease apart.

The generally accepted trigger for everything was the sudden rupture of a blind-thrust fault at depth oriented approximately north–south, close to Charing Cross. Almost immediately it activated the sleeping and previously unknown Greendale Fault further south, ripping open a nearly 30km-long gash across the plains that offset shelter belts, roads and railway lines.

Another northeast–southwest-lying blind-thrust fault to the southwest of Hororata is then thought to have snapped underground, followed quickly by what some researchers think may have been the breaking of a fourth fault of similar kind and orientation running somewhere on a line from West Melton to Sandy Knolls to Burnham.

The angry rumble of the quakes roared across the plains ahead of the ground shaking, as the primary (or 'P') waves largely responsible for the sound separated from the slower secondary (or 'S' waves) even slower ground waves that cause the ground motion. Christchurch residents likened the swelling noise to that of an approaching locomotive engine or a Boeing 747. Once the S waves arrived, the city shook and then rolled heavily for 30 seconds or more and the power went off. Harrowing aftershocks began just minutes later as the wobbling ground started the long process of trying to revert to some kind of equilibrium.

Two GNS Science seismologists have attempted since to separate the events

using geological observations, GPS (global positioning system) calculations and satellite radar images, strong motion records and computer modelling. Dr Caroline Holden's original model for three quakes, which she is still refining, is that the recording of a 7.1-magnitude quake can be accounted for by an about 6.3-magnitude quake lasting two to four seconds on the Charing Cross fault, followed by a 6.9 shake lasting seven to 18 seconds on the Greendale Fault and a close-to-6.5 jolt of 15 to 18 seconds near Hororata.

Her colleague Dr John Beavan is more convinced that a fourth fault exists and does not rule out further faults. His original calculation of the rupture sequence is slightly different, putting the initial quake at magnitude 6.5, followed by shakes of 7 and 6.2 on the second and third faults and a last rupture on the fourth of about 6.5.

Scientists initially told the many fearful Cantabrians that the frequent nerve-wracking aftershocks were likely to continue for weeks, perhaps months. Not long after, that warning was confirmed to be months, and possibly a year or more. Seismologists also used Bath's Law — which states that the average difference in magnitude between a mainshock and its largest aftershock is 1.2 — to forecast a possible magnitude 6 aftershock. But as weeks, then months, went by, the chance of that happening seemed to fade and largely dropped out of the public's mind.

At the same time, aftershock-weary

ABOVE: *The fault line which ruptured in Canterbury's 4 September 2010 earthquake. The fault runs across the paddocks and road.* PHOTO: RICHARD COSGROVE

residents quickly became used to quakes of anything less than magnitude 5, only really sitting up and taking notice once they exceeded that level. One of those gave a hint of the terrible events to come on 22 February, but of course its significance could not possibly be grasped at the time.

On Wednesday 8 September at 7.49am, the people of Lyttelton, Heathcote and the eastern Port Hills suburbs of Mount Pleasant and Redcliffs were shaken up badly by a magnitude 5 quake that was only 6.5km deep but centred below the hills close to the Lyttelton road tunnel. Residents reported the quake as quite violent, with 150 people rating it on the GeoNet site as a 6 (slightly damaging) or 7 (damaging) on the Modified Mercalli scale. In fact, many, including some Civil Defence people, thought it was the magnitude 6 that had been predicted. As it happened, while it was still an aftershock of 4 September, it also turned out to be a foreshock for 22 February. It tipped off scientists to a fault below the hills, but the significance of that can only be appreciated with hindsight.

Aftershocks continued through October and November and died away in December, before suddenly firing up again on Boxing Day. It was a day of heightened seismic activity that peaked in the damaging magnitude 4.9 quake at 10.30am, the result of another very shallow rupture on yet another previously unknown fault, this time almost directly under central Christchurch. Frightened central-city shoppers who seconds before had been enjoying the

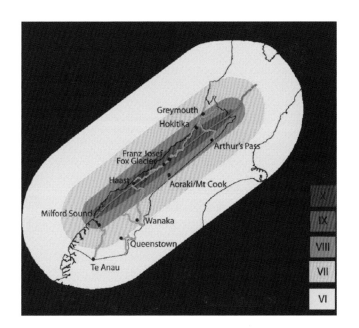

Boxing Day sales rushed into the streets, and buildings that had been damaged in September swayed and crumbled further, leading to many more receiving the Civil Defence red stickers that said they were unsafe until engineers decided otherwise.

The aftershocks died away the following day as quickly as they had begun, and Christchurch then enjoyed a much more stable period through January, despite a magnitude 5.1 quake on 20 January.

At the start of February, GNS Science issued a revised forecast of likely aftershock sizes and said there was still a 25 per cent chance of a magnitude 6 or higher quake in the Christchurch and central Canterbury region over the next year. That warning was not widely disseminated or absorbed. Sadly it was only three weeks later that those seemingly remote-enough odds came to pass.

ABOVE: *Expected Modified Mercalli shaking with a major rupture of the Alpine Fault. The Modified Mercalli Scale is a subjective measure of how intensely people feel the shaking from an earthquake.*

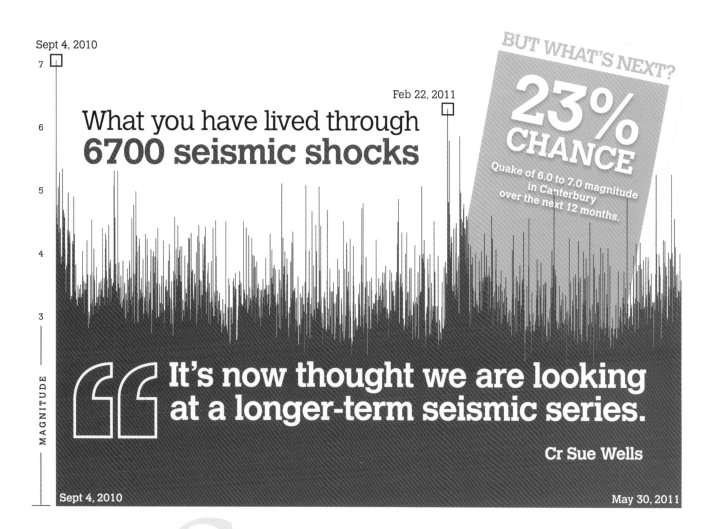

Sept 4, 2010

7

6

Feb 22, 2011

What you have lived through
6700 seismic shocks

5

BUT WHAT'S NEXT?

23%
CHANCE

Quake of 6.0 to 7.0 magnitude
in Canterbury
over the next 12 months.

4

3

MAGNITUDE

" It's now thought we are looking at a longer-term seismic series.

Cr Sue Wells

Sept 4, 2010   May 30, 2011

Christchurch woke to a drizzly, cool and gloomy morning on Tuesday 22 February. All day, a persistent grey veil of low cloud hung sullenly over the city. Christchurch folk in every suburb went about their daily grind, the ever-present risk of aftershocks an accepted threat but, for many, one that had become hidden some way in the sub-conscious.

Under the Port Hills, the fault that revealed a glimpse of its violent character on 8 September was about to rip open and generate a magnitude 6.343 quake, which would combine devastingly with the city's unusual geology to make Christchurch one of the unluckiest cities in the world.

Analysis by GNS Science shows the fault rupture began shortly before 12.51pm and 43 seconds, with a small amount of slip between the two sides of the fault about 7km

underground. Over the next few seconds, the rupture propagated upwards and towards the northwest, with the amount of movement across the fault increasing. The largest amount of slip, around 1.5m, occurred between about 3km and 5km deep. The angle of the fault, dipping down towards the southeast beneath the hills, meant it was effectively pointing back directly at Christchurch to the northwest when it broke, releasing about 42,000 tonnes of energy straight at the city.

The first waves from the quake felt to many like just another large aftershock, but within only two to three seconds all hell broke loose across the city and the quake's true nature became frightfully clear.

GNS Science seismologist Dr Bill Fry says the savage and unprecedented (in New Zealand) levels of ground-shaking, unusually

SEPTEMBER

4.35am - 7.1 magnitude

04.09.10

After the September earthquake, Christchurch roads received a hammering but it was largely isolated to a few heavily hit suburbs such as Halswell, Bexley and Avonside.

1200
ROAD REPAIRS

Christchurch roads are in a sorry state after the February earthquake. Photo: KIRK HARGREAVES

ABOVE: *The intensity of the shaking on 22 February is reflected in the amount of liquefaction and road damage in the city's eastern suburbs compared with that of 4 September, as seen in this graphic.*

FEBRUARY
22.02.11

The damage encompasses the entire eastern side of Christchurch. Major arterial routes and the four avenues around the central city were badly damaged.

38,000
ROAD REPAIRS

STYX
REDWOOD
CASEBROOK
MARSHLAND
PARKLANDS
NORTH SHORE
BISHOPDALE
NORTHCOTE
WAIMAIRI BEACH
PAPANUI
BURWOOD
NORTH NEW BRIGHTON
BRYNDWR
WESTHAVEN
SHIRLEY
MAIREHAU
NEW BRIGHTON
ST ALBANS
AVONDALE
MERIVALE
DALLINGTON
BEXLEY
FENDALTON
RICHMOND
WAINONI
ILAM
ARANUI
AVONSIDE
NORTH LINWOOD
UPPER RICCARTON
RICCARTON
SOUTH NEW BRIGHTON
LINWOOD
BROMLEY
MIDDLETON
PHILIPSTOWN
ADDINGTON
SYDENHAM
CHARLESTON
SOUTHSHORE
SPREYDON
WALTHAM
WOOLSTON
SOMERFIELD
FERRYMEAD
ST ANDREWS HILL
REDCLIFFS
HOON HAY
MURRAY AYNSLEY
HILLSBOROUGH
MT. PLEASANT
MONCKS BAY
HUNTSBURY
CLIFTON
HEATHCOTE VALLEY
RICHMOND HILL
SUMNER
CRACROFT
CASHMERE
WESTMORLAND
TAYLORS MISTAKE
HALSWELL
RAPAKI
CASS BAY
CORSAIR BAY
LYTTELTON
GOVERNORS BAY

high energy release, the angle of the fault pointing at the city like a loaded gun, and the trampoline-like bouncing of ground layers under the city combined over 15 to 20 seconds to wreak havoc at the surface. A monitoring station in the Heathcote valley recorded ground accelerations upwards equal to 2.2 times that of gravity just a few seconds into the quake.

Fry says the Port Hills Fault and the faults that broke on 4 September were unusually strong.

'When a strong fault breaks it releases more energy than an equal-sized weak fault. Think about the difference between breaking a 1cm-thick sheet of styrofoam and a 1cm-thick sheet of plywood, and the amount of jarring you would feel in your hands. The Canterbury crust is like the plywood, but most earthquakes are more like breaking the styrofoam.'

That fault strength was also a factor behind the speed of the rupture, which was faster than for most quakes of the same magnitude. While the ground-breaking along the fault only lasted about three seconds, because of its speed people in the city were feeling the first waves from the shake before the rupture had even finished. The ground-shaking was especially violent due to the waves from the rupture, and the rupture itself, moving in the same direction.

'It's like bulldozing snow. You are pushing snow along that you've already collected, but all the time you are adding more,' Fry says.

When the earthquake hit, the weaker top few metres of ground under the city

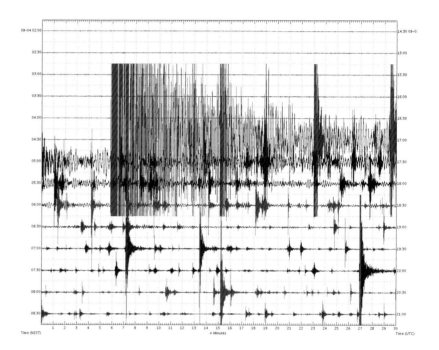

'trampolined' further upwards than stronger layers lower down and separated from them, an effect that scientists have only recently discovered. The February quake will provide scientists with a full set of data to study the effect more closely.

'When these upper layers fell back under gravity, they "slapped" against the lower layers coming up again, producing very high impacts. Think of jumping on a trampoline. If you change the rate at which you jump, and get out of synch with the trampoline, when you come down and land as the trampoline is still heading upwards, you get quite a jolt to your knees.'

As buildings disintegrated, crushing and trapping people — more than 180 fatally — choking billows of dust filled the streets and rose up towards the heavy clouds lowering

ABOVE: *GeoNet seismogram for the 7.1 earthquake, 4 September 2010.*

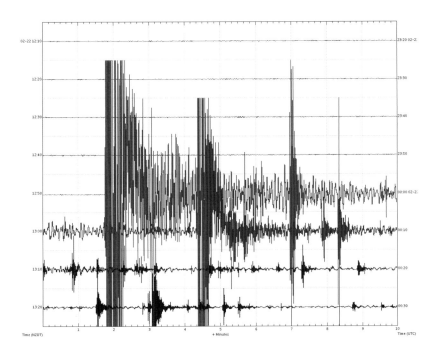

ABOVE: *GeoNet seismogram for the 6.3 earthquake, 22 February 2011 (note the difference in scale).*

over the shocked city. A major magnitude 5.845 aftershock brought down more masonry only 13 minutes later, followed at 2.50pm by an even larger 5.91 quake. Between the 6.343 and the 5.91 there were another 22 aftershocks of more than magnitude 4, seven of them between magnitude 4.5 and 5.

The ground hardly stopped shaking in the first hour after the killer quake, with nine shakes of more than magnitude 4 — including a 4.839, 4.863 and 4.807 — in the first eight minutes after the first quake. In all, there were 46 aftershocks of at least magnitude 4 in the 24 hours after the big quake, including a magnitude 5.011 at 4.04pm.

Vast amounts of energy were released in the first few hours, changing the shape of Christchurch. The Port Hills are 40cm taller in places as a result of the colossal forces unleashed, and Lyttelton is now several centimetres closer to the city.

Satellite analysis by GNS Science shows the top of the roughly east–west buried Port Hills Fault lies between 1km and 2km below the southern edge of the Avon–Heathcote Estuary. Land on either side of the fault has slipped horizontally as well as vertically, with places south of the estuary shifting west by a few tens of centimetres while land north of it has moved a similar amount to the east.

Teams of scientists have begun sifting through records of the day and investigating more closely what else may lie under Christchurch to ensure the rebuilt city is robust enough to cope with the future level of earthquake risk. There will be more to come.

As buildings disintegrated, crushing and trapping people — more than180 fatally — choking billows of dust filled the streets and rose up towards the heavy clouds lowering over the shocked city. A major magnitude 5.845 aftershock brought down more masonry only 13 minutes later, followed at 2.50pm by an even larger 5.91 quake.

Christchurch's Red Zone shortly after 22 February

CRITICAL BUILDINGS

Christchurch CBD buildings that will probably have to come down:

1. Rolleston Courts Apts
35 Cambridge Tce
....
2. NZ College of Early Childhood Education
50 Victoria St
....
3. Community House
141 Hereford St
....
4. BDO Spicer House
148 Victoria St
....
5. Hotel Grand Chancellor
161 Cashel St
....
6. Harcourts Grenadier
271 Madras St
....
7. Kenton Chambers
190-192 Hereford St

DROP ZONES

Authorities also released details of the "drop zones" around damaged high rise buildings in the central business district.

Engineers believe if the buildings were to collapse, they would fall within the marked zone.

Fears of collapse have frustrated business owners, desperate to gain access to valuable property in the central business district.

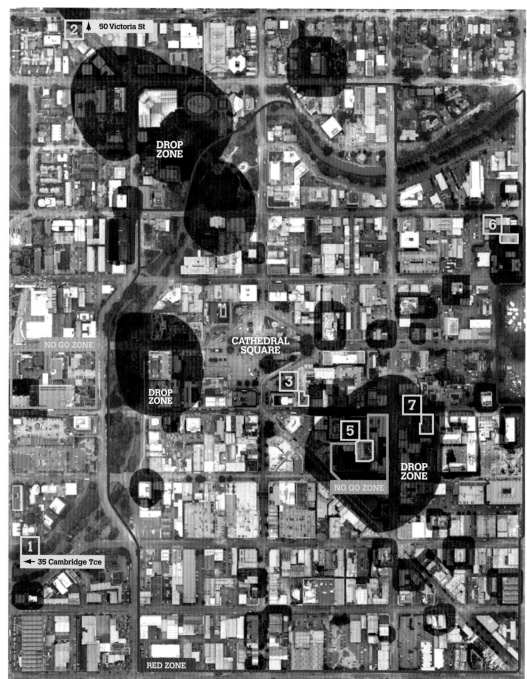

Largest aftershocks since 22 February

over magnitude 4.5 on the Richter scale

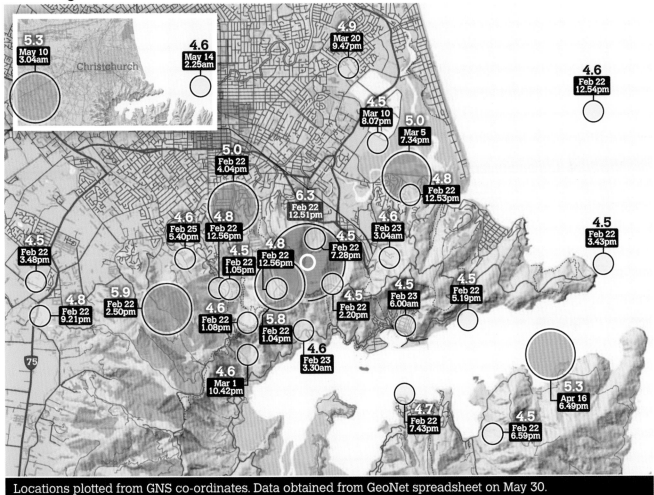

Locations plotted from GNS co-ordinates. Data obtained from GeoNet spreadsheet on May 30.

Vast amounts of energy were released in the first few hours, changing the shape of Christchurch. The Port Hills are 40cm taller in places as a result of the colossal forces unleashed, and Lyttelton is now several centimetres closer to the city.

LEFT: *The New Zealand armed forces played a major role in rescue and relief operations following the earthquake. In Lyttelton, the commander of joint forces, Air Vice Marshall Peter Stockwell and Chief of Army, Tim Keating, were briefed against the backdrop of the HMNZS Canterbury.*

PHOTO: CPL SAM SHEPHERD
NEW ZEALAND DEFENCE FORCE

The Rescuers

Chris Moore

OPPOSITE: *Christchurch became the focus of a major international relief operation. This unidentified rescue worker from Queensland was photographed at the collapsed Canterbury Television building.*

PHOTO: REUTERS

They came from throughout New Zealand and the world: an army of 900 men and women who reacted to a city's need with energy, endurance and dedication. The international search and rescue teams who responded so quickly to Christchurch's plight became our Samaritans and heroes as they painstakingly searched the rubble and debris for the trapped and injured, and recovered our dead with compassion.

How they came to be here within hours of the earthquake is not simply the story of a major international relief effort — it is also a story of generosity, compassion and co-operation.

Within hours of the earthquake, the New Zealand government signed off emergency spending powers to facilitate the rescue of those trapped in the rubble.

'Time is now going to be of the essence,' Deputy Prime Minister Bill English warned, after taking the rare step of signing special approval for emergency spending under the Public Finance Act.

Within hours of the declaration of a state of emergency, Christchurch became the focus of a major international relief programme. The New Zealand Defence Force had been performing a major military exercise in Oamaru and Timaru and immediately deployed up to 1000 personnel. Air force helicopters were flown from Ohakea, while the navy's

ABOVE: *Troops from the 3rd Field Engineers, Royal New Zealand Army, provided fresh water and supplies for residents at New Brighton.*

PHOTO: NEW ZEALAND DEFENCE FORCE

multi-role ship HMNZS *Canterbury*, together with the naval vessels *Otago*, *Resolution* and *Pukaki*, had all been based in Lyttelton during the earthquake. Additional firefighters and paramedics from throughout the country were also deployed, and police readied a large number of officers. As darkness fell over the shattered central city and suburbs, Canterbury District Police commander Superintendent Dave Cliff said a 'large number' of police would assist the urban search and rescue teams who had already settled in for the long haul.

The mounting pressure on the emergency services was illustrated when Christchurch's St John Ambulance brigade reported that it had received 353 calls

within the first two hours of the quake.

More than 30 ambulance staff flew from Auckland to help, along with ambulances and staff from other centres. St John sent three helicopters from Dunedin with two clinical staff and equipment on each one. A helicopter also left Wellington carrying four Wellington Free Ambulance staff.

The Fire Service sent its two North Island urban search and rescue task forces on flights from Ohakea to support its Christchurch team. Several fire engines and 20 firefighters and other staff travelled from Dunedin and Invercargill in the 'first wave' of support. National commander Mike Hall said the service was responding with all its resources, and crews from other parts of the country also soon arrived.

LEFT: *New Zealand defence personnel on patrol in the streets of Lyttelton shortly after the earthquake severely damaged buildings and infrastructure in the historic port town.*

PHOTO: KIRK HARGREAVES

BELOW: *Medical teams joined ambulance staff and rescue teams to treat the injured at the PGC building on Cambridge Terrace.*

PHOTO: JOHN KIRK-ANDERSON

LEFT: *A reassuring smile from First Sergeant Rahim, Singapore Armed Forces, on duty in Bealey Avenue outside Knox Church.*

PHOTO: ANDREW GORRIE

LEFT: *Evacuees from Christchurch on board an RNZAF Hercules during the emergency relief operation.*

PHOTO: NEW ZEALAND DEFENCE FORCE

OPPOSITE: *The Royal New Zealand Navy was in port and on hand to take part in the disaster relief operation. In Lyttelton, naval personnel from HMNZS Canterbury delivered food to the Diamond Harbour wharf.*

PHOTO: KIRK HARGREAVES

ABOVE: *On the front line — members of the Disaster Victims Identification team at Burnham Camp faced the human reality of the disaster. From left: Barry Shepherd (mortuary post-mortem); Al Hendrickson (administration manager); Richard McPhail (mortuary co-ordinator); Dr Simon Stables (lead forensic pathologist) and Gordon Matenga (acting chief coroner).*

PHOTO: ANDREW GORRIE

The world responded to Christchurch's plight within hours of the earthquake. Members of the New South Wales Police were among the first to arrive at Christchurch Airport. PHOTO: PETER MEECHAM

Australian urban search and rescue teams totalling 142 personnel and three dogs, a disaster medical assistance team of 23 emergency and surgical personnel and a 75-bed field hospital arrived. Three hundred Australian police officers came to help with security around the Christchurch city centre.

ABOVE: *Assessing the damage — Defence Force medical staff in central Christchurch. From left: Warren Officer Class 1 Tim Crowe; Royal New Zealand Army medical director Lt Colonel Andrew Dunn and Major Brendan Wood in the field.*
PHOTO: PETER DRURY

RIGHT: *Co-operation in a disaster — New Zealand Defence Force personnel assisted police in providing cordon support in the central business district.*
PHOTO: NEW ZEALAND DEFENCE FORCE

The New Zealand teams were soon joined by international crews. Two Australian urban search and rescue teams totalling 142 personnel (72 from New South Wales and 70 Queenslanders) and three dogs, a disaster medical assistance team of 23 emergency and surgical personnel and a 75-bed field hospital arrived. Three hundred Australian police officers came to help with security around the Christchurch city centre.

An urban search and rescue team of 67 personnel with three dogs came from Japan, joining a Taiwanese team of 24 personnel with two dogs.

Singapore dispatched a rescue team of 55 people and four dogs, plus 116 Singaporean defence force personnel who also assisted with the security cordon around central

LEFT: *There were lighter moments during the relief operation and the days following the 22 February earthquake. Earthquake 'Doctor' Exami Nation helped to lighten the load of emergency workers, including Roger Cliffe from Wellington's Victoria University.*

PHOTO: ANDREW GORRIE

OPPOSITE TOP: *Members of the Taiwanese search and rescue team prepare to enter a Montreal Street building two days after the earthquake. They were part of an international disaster relief operation which saw emergency workers from throughout the world arriving in the city.*

PHOTO: MARTIN DE RUYTER

OPPOSITE: *A sorrow shared — the team from the Los Angeles Fire Department search and rescue unit observe the national two-minute silence in memory of the victims of the earthquake.*

PHOTO: PETER DRURY

Christchurch. Two Singaporean C130 aircraft were also made available to transport evacuees from Christchurch to Auckland.

The United Kingdom initially sent six fire service search and rescue experts, the advance party of a 55-member urban search and rescue team.

An urban search and rescue team travelled from the United States with 80 personnel, plus 40 tonnes of equipment.

Christchurch mayor Bob Parker said words could not describe how grateful the city was for the overseas help.

'It means absolutely everything. To have people from many nations coming here to help this city is deeply moving and deeply supportive for all of us, and we thank you

from the bottom of our hearts.'

As the first day ended, the nation was told that the official death toll stood at 65 but, experts warned, would increase.

'In the last few hours the scale of the destruction has become increasingly apparent, as has the scale of the potential loss of life. I've just spoken to the Prime Minister, who's emphasised the utter devastation that he has seen there and described the ongoing aftershocks as violent,' Bill English told a second emergency Cabinet meeting.

Christchurch Hospital was still operational and an emergency operations centre was being set up at Princess Margaret Hospital. Other South Island hospitals had been cleared to take casualties. Defence force personnel

LEFT: *Japanese rescue workers walk past the ruins of the Canterbury Television building as recovery teams intensified their search for survivors of the 22 February earthquake. But hopes were rapidly fading as the rescue operation became a recovery exercise.*
PHOTO: REUTERS

BELOW: *They came to the most English of New Zealand cities to help in the earthquake relief operation. The United Kingdom's Fire Service International Rescue Team are pictured after its arrival at Christchurch Airport.* PHOTO: DEREK FLYNN

ABOVE: *Shortly after hearing news of the Christchurch earthquake, members of the Palmerston North-based Urban Search and Rescue Task Force One were on duty and preparing to travel south to take part in the relief operations.*

PHOTO: ROBERT KITCHIN

'It means absolutely everything. To have people from many nations coming here to help this city is deeply moving and deeply supportive for all of us, and we thank you from the bottom of our hearts.'

— Christchurch mayor Bob Parker

LEFT: *As the world's media focused on Christchurch and the continuing effects of the earthquake, communications became a vital part of the relief operation. Here search and rescue co-ordinator Jim Stuart Black talks at the regular afternoon briefings. Behind him Christchurch's mayor, Bob Parker, listens.*

PHOTO: CHRIS HILLOCK

were also providing medical assistance around the city and medical staff were being brought in from around the country to help, including nurses with specialist intensive-care skills.

The confirmed death toll rose steadily. The global impact of the disaster became clearer as Foreign Affairs Minister Murray McCully revealed that international visitors including Chinese, Japanese, Taiwanese, Filipinos and Britons were believed to be among the dead.

McCully told foreign diplomats that over the next few days many overseas families would have to be told 'very bad news'.

'I can say clearly this is not just New Zealand's tragedy,' he said.

On the ground, rain and a succession of aftershocks added to the mammoth task facing the rescue workers, and made some damaged buildings even more unstable.

Earthquake Recovery Minister Gerry Brownlee also had stark news for Christchurch. It would cost more than $10 billion to rebuild the quake-ravaged city.

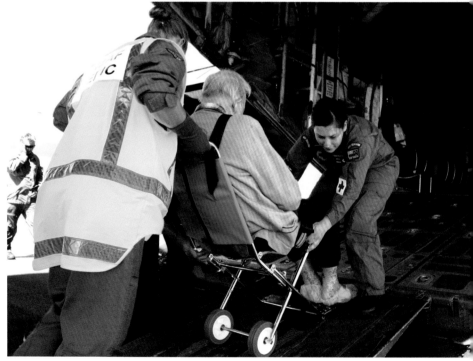

ABOVE: *Many elderly people, including residents of damaged rest homes throughout the city, were evacuated to other centres after the earthquake. Passengers on this Royal New Zealand Air Force Hercules flight from Christchurch arrived in Nelson where they were helped from the plane by air force and St Johns Ambulance personnel.* PHOTO: BRANDON KAY

ABOVE: *The Disaster Victims Identification team works at the Pyne Gould Corporation building. The DVI's operations involved a painstaking search of any building or area where people died during the earthquake.*

PHOTO: PHIL REID

RIGHT: *Search and rescue team members applaud as a man is rescued alive from the Pyne Gould Corporation building.*

PHOTO: BLAIR ENSOR

ABOVE LEFT: *A member of Queensland's search and rescue team at work in central Christchurch in the aftermath of the February earthquake.*

PHOTO: PHIL REID

The Earthquake Commission had received 181,000 claims after the 4 September tremor and another 130,000 were expected after the February quake, 'making it one of the biggest insurance events in the world'.

The government also announced that it was cancelling the census scheduled for 8 March. It was not the time to be going door to door asking New Zealanders for information, it added.

Thousands of Christchurch residents would flee the city following the earthquake. For some, it would be weeks or months before they returned — others said they would never come back. Christchurch Airport estimated that as many as 12,000 additional passengers had flown out of the city in the first week.

For those left behind — many living without power or water — conditions began to slowly improve during the weeks after the tremor shattered their lives. Around 2000 portable toilets, including some from the United States, were distributed around the city. Fresh water was trucked in to parts of the city still without water supply and army engineers set up a desalination plant in New Brighton to produce 2000 litres of fresh water an hour. Community laundries were set up in the city and the surrounding areas.

While Orion painstakingly worked to restore power to Christchurch, they warned that it could take weeks to restore power to about 50,000 customers in Dallington, New Brighton and Sumner.

Telecom staff also focused on restoring

ABOVE: *Members of the United States rescue team take a well-earned break from their operations in the central city.*

PHOTO: REUTERS

phone lines, installing 60 generators to provide back-up power to network sites still without mains power. Telecom collected analogue landline phones for distribution to those without electricity.

More than two-thirds of the city's pharmacies reopened within days of the earthquake, but soon began to run out of medications and other supplies. The

warehouse of a Christchurch medicine supplier remained closed, while a second was able to provide only limited services.

But as medical supplies dwindled, busy doctors and nurses were bolstered by the arrival of hundreds of primary-care professionals. More than 600 general practitioners and practice nurses volunteered their services in Christchurch and other

areas that saw an influx of patients due to the earthquake.

Then there was Christchurch's Student Army. Coordinated by law student Sam Johnson, the 800-strong force of student volunteers armed with spades, wheelbarrows, high spirits and an apparently inexhaustible supply of energy hit suburban streets to begin shovelling tonnes of smelly silt from back yards. The volunteer army nearly doubled in size as it moved into Dallington, Avonside and Avondale.

Ten days after the quake, Christchurch was officially moving from a rescue to a recovery mission. But the pain and grief remained.

'We now face the reality that there is no chance that anyone could have survived this long. Efforts have to shift to the recovery of loved ones and their return to their families,' Civil Defence national controller John Hamilton said.

'So far, we know that 161 lives have been lost. People from up to 20 countries will be among the final, tragic death toll, which will probably end up somewhere around 220.

'We need to be realistic and we need to help families through what is now a grim reality,' said Hamilton.

ABOVE: *Team members from the Hanmer Springs Volunteer Fire Brigade work on temporary repairs to the roof of Bruce Hood's Heathcote home. Hanmer Springs personnel worked in the Pyne Gould Corporation building before helping Christchurch residents get back on their feet.*
PHOTO: DEREK FLYYN

LEFT: *Mark (right) and Paul Lupi (centre), volunteers in safety vests from the Rangiora Response Unit, distribute clean water to residents.*

PHOTO: REUTERS

RIGHT: *Tania Jones of Nelson-based New Zealand Response Team 2 searches buildings and abandoned vehicles in Colombo Street.*

PHOTO: MARTIN DE RUYTER

LEFT: *The New Zealand Urban Search and Rescue team in the ravaged interior of Christ Church Cathedral. The cathedral's tower and spire collapsed across the end of the nave during February's earthquake, breaking a beating and vital heart of the Christchurch community. Despite earlier fears that at least 20 people may have been killed, a search of the building eventually found no bodies.*

PHOTO: SARAH IVEY

OPPOSITE TOP: *Two tourists speak to a police officer and two soldiers from New Zealand and Singapore at a cordon into the central city. Christchurch's central business district remained sealed off for several weeks before the cordon slowly shrank and people were allowed back into some areas. In June 2011, some sections of the CBD still lay behind barriers.*

PHOTO: JOHN KIRK-ANDERSON

RIGHT: *Thank you! Armed forces personnel delivered food to Christchurch people affected by the earthquake. In Dallington Terrace, one soldier is hugged by a grateful resident.*

PHOTO: RICHARD COSGROVE

LEFT: *Shrouded in dust, an emergency worker toils in the rubble and debris of the CTV building two days after the 22 February earthquake. Efforts to locate survivors continued despite fading hopes of finding any more people alive in the ruins.*
PHOTO: REUTERS

RIGHT: *Focusing on hope — two members of the search and rescue teams survey the continuing operation in the Pyne Gould Corporation building.*
PHOTO: CHRIS SKELTON

Rescue teams had rescued 70 people alive from collapsed buildings, but the last survivor came out a little over 24 hours after the earthquake. The international standard for finding survivors is usually within 72 hours.

The change of approach by rescue workers meant that teams started to carefully 'deconstruct' what was left of the broken buildings. Many, previously accessed only by search dogs and cameras, contained sections that had not been searched.

Most of the collapsed buildings were lifted open and 'unpicked' with heavy machinery that had stayed away while there was still the prospect of finding survivors inside. At a handful of sites, including the PGC and Canterbury Television buildings and the Christ Church Cathedral, work carried on as before, but the hope of finding survivors became slimmer by the hour.

'It is highly, highly unlikely that we will encounter anybody who is alive,' fire service national manager for special operations Jim Stuart-Black said.

'But clearly, there is an occasional miracle so we conduct our operations to allow for that miracle.' Care was also important, considering the certainty that there would be further bodies to emerge from the wreckage, he added.

Mayor Bob Parker also acknowledged that any hope for survivors had all but disappeared.

'The reality is that a decision had to be made. It is part of being honest and open and giving clarity to this situation that we're in,' Parker said.

Prime Minister John Key again paid tribute to the rescuers' efforts.

'To everyone involved in the rescue effort from here and overseas, can I extend the country's thanks for your tireless efforts in what has been a very difficult and dangerous environment. There have been many stories of courage and bravery and I'm sure that many more will emerge over the coming days.'

CIVIL DEFENCE

t The state of national emergency declared shortly after the February earthquake struck Christchurch was the first time in New Zealand's history that it had been invoked for a Civil Defence emergency. The only other time a state of national emergency had been previously declared was during the 1951 waterfront workers' strike.

In a ministerial statement to Parliament, Minister of Civil Defence John Carter said the emergency was of 'such a degree that the required Civil Defence emergency management will be beyond the capacity of local Civil Defence emergency people to respond on their own'.

The existing Civil Defence Emergency Management Act says declared emergencies have a seven-day duration, and may be extended or terminated. It gives Civil Defence personnel the power to close and restrict access to roads and public places; remove and secure dangerous structures and materials; provide rescue, first aid, food and shelter; conserve essential supplies and regulate traffic; dispose of dead people and animals; advise the public; provide equipment; enter and evacuate premises; remove vehicles; and requisition equipment and materials or assistance.

A state of national emergency was not declared for previous disasters, including the 1931 7.8-magnitude Napier earthquake, which killed 256 people. Carter said it was justified in this case because of the devastation and the likely impact on so many people.

The head of the Civil Defence effort was John Hamilton, the director of the Ministry of Civil Defence and Emergency Management. Hamilton faced a huge challenge taking on the job. 'I always knew we would go through an adrenaline rush at the start. Everyone works hard with huge effort and willpower, but they run out of puff after a while, and then it slowly starts to become frustration to get things completed,' he said.

'I'm not going to do something that jeopardises people's lives. We've had enough of that,' he added. 'I understand people's frustrations . . . but I'm not prepared to put people in harm's way.

'Unless you have been there [in the red zone] and seen it, you don't know what you are missing. I don't want to be the guy that let somebody into a dicey area to find they get injured. I don't want that to happen.'

Hamilton said he would stay in charge until the city was 'stabilised' and the extraordinary

powers granted in the wake of the earthquake were no longer required.

'To me, it is when people are housed in one way or another, that they are warm and dry, that there is access to services — water, power, telecommunications especially — that there are safe roads, the beginnings or positive signs of business activity in the city, the size of the cordon has been reduced to an absolute minimum, schools are back operating and, ultimately, there is a plan in place for a full-blown recovery.' He would later hand over authority to the Canterbury Earthquake Recovery Authority (CERA) on 30 April.

ABOVE: *John Hamilton stands in Manchester Street during a media tour of the Red Zone.*

PHOTO: JOHN KIRK-ANDERSON

The Volunteers

LEFT: *Class photo — members of Christchurch's Student Volunteer Army assemble, shovels and wheelbarrows at the ready, before setting out on another day's operation to help the people of Christchurch recover from the earthquake.*

PHOTO: ANDREW GORRIE

ABOVE: *Country and town — The Farmy Army is here. The Federated Farmers initiative saw a tide of volunteers arrive in Christchurch to help in the continuing clean-up exercise.*

PHOTO: CRAIG SIMCOX

University students sometimes get a bad rap: they are most likely to be seen on the television news partying, living in squalid flats or protesting about fee rises. But in the wake of the devastating quake, thousands of students put down their beers and books to lend a hand to those in need.

Christchurch's Student Volunteer Army was formed after the 4 September earthquake, when hundreds of Canterbury University students helped residents to clean up silt in the worst-affected suburbs. Group founder Sam Johnson said more than 3000 students had taken part in the volunteer effort.

An administrative team of 100 people co-ordinated the effort, with volunteers working through sections of the city 'quite methodically' to ensure that work was completed as quickly as possible. Group members met regularly with Civil Defence, Fulton Hogan and City Care, who were in charge of clean-up and continuing stabilisation and restoration, to determine which parts of the city they should visit.

'Instead of having five people spending a day on one property, we have 20 people spending one or two hours — it's a big morale-booster.'

Johnson said the group had received donations of food and supplies from all over the country, as well as a $20,000 grant from the Ministry of Youth Development.

Organisers also worked to keep volunteers motivated, so they would keep going for as long as possible.

RIGHT: *The pink-shirted Comfort Crusaders also played their part. Volunteers spread good cheer, home baking, essential supplies and even hugs to lighten the load in the days following the earthquake. From left: Melissa Thacker, Brian Thorne, Amanda Keefe, Chris Jack; Front: Petrina Chai, Jack Fletcher.*

PHOTO: BRUCE MERCER

BELOW RIGHT: *A helping hand — Sam Johnson, the man behind the establishment of Christchurch's Student Volunteer Army.*

'We can't let people get too bogged down in the emotional side of it. If we want to keep them volunteering, they need to enjoy themselves,' he said.

The 21-year-old Canterbury University law and political science student is seen by John Key as a future prime minister. Active in the university's Student Volunteer network, Johnson has been involved in the revival of the musical theatre society, setting up a University Performing Arts Association and organising inter-university exchanges. He said his leadership of the volunteering effort was based on his belief that more young people needed to be involved in the community.

'We had a week off uni with nothing to do, so why not get involved? There were a lot of people organising parties on Facebook, but I thought we could do better than that.'

Johnson said he wanted to focus on improving inter-generational activity and neighbourhood relations.

'If you get to know the people living next door to you, you can treat them with some sort of decency, particularly in the student areas.'

The students were not alone. Following the February quake, the Farmy Army (which had been formed after the September shock), once again mobilised to help its urban cousins clean up Christchurch.

Just as the students got together in their thousands to rid Christchurch properties of the silt brought up by earthquake liquefaction, farmers and other rural people pitched in to help city dwellers get through the hard slog.

The efforts of the Farmy Army were co-ordinated by Federated Farmers, with Canterbury Agricultural Park as its headquarters. In a literal call to arms, farmers were asked to supply muscle power, as well as mini-diggers, loaders and trailers to remove material.

Federated Farmers estimates that since the earthquake 4000 volunteers, including farmers and rural contractors, have helped to remove 70,000 cubic metres of silt, involving 28,000 hours of digging on top of another 28,000 machine hours.

The speedy provision of water was brought about by rural companies delivering

ABOVE: *Volunteers from throughout New Zealand joined a church-based operation to distribute food parcels throughout Christchurch. A large distribution warehouse in Halswell became the base for the group's work.*

PHOTO: BRUCE MERCER

LEFT: *Volunteer members of the Farmy Army help residents of Cresselly Place, St Martins, clear the effects of liquefaction from their street and homes.*

PHOTO: KEVIN STENT

approximately 5.5 million litres from Silver Fern Farms' (SFF) Islington reservoir to Christchurch, including to hospitals and emergency services which initially ran low on water.

Farmers were also asked to donate meat and wool in a 'meat the needs of Christchurch' campaign by the federation through eight meat and two wool companies. The campaign was kick-started by Waikato meat processor Greenlea Premier Meats and its staff making a $150,000 donation, followed by SFF and its international partners donating $600,000 to the overall earthquake appeal.

The federation's earthquake spokesman,

John Hartnell, said many farmers around the country who were unable to visit Christchurch to help had pledged livestock to a charitable trust set up for the meat campaign.

Farmers had provided their time and equipment generously because they felt for people whose homes had been wrecked, he said.

'Most of the fuel has been funded by farmers providing machinery. We have a fuel tank to fill up diggers, but none has gone into vehicles.

'I don't know how you add that up, and it's been an enormous effort.'

PREVIOUS PAGES: *Team talk — Dem Doroschenko discusses tactics with the Student Volunteer Army in Avondale before the volunteers confront the job at hand — clearing the sea of silt caused by liquefaction.*

PHOTO: COLIN SMITH

ABOVE: *Shovels firmly in hand, the Student Volunteer Army walks into the Christchurch suburb of Avonside to clear silt and sand from footpaths and roads.* PHOTO: COLIN SMITH

LEFT: *Volunteers from the Federated Farmers of New Zealand shovel mud that flowed from the ground as a result of the earthquake, on a residential street in central Christchurch.*

PHOTO: REUTERS

RIGHT: *Cashmere High School placed its call for help to clear its playing fields of mud on the internet. A small army of volunteers arrived to assist, including Jamie Hunt (right) and Brodie Hyland.*

PHOTO: CHRIS HILLOCK

LEFT: *Have wheelbarrow, will travel — Tom Nation from the Student Volunteer Army works at Seabreeze Close, Bexley.*

PHOTO: KIRK HARGREAVES

OPPOSITE: *A constant stream of trucks transport tonnes of silt caused by liquefaction to a landfill site at Burwood.*

PHOTO: CRAIG SIMCOX

RIGHT: *Two members of the Student Volunteer Army, Ben Wortelboer (left) and Nick Hand (right) negotiate damaged roads and dust to help in the massive clean-up after the earthquake. At one point, nearly 800 people were working with the SVA.*

PHOTO: DEREK FLYNN

LEFT: *As the aftershocks continued into April, John Gordon surveys the liquefaction in the driveway of his Bexley home once again — and contemplates yet another clean-up.*

PHOTO: DON SCOTT

ABOVE: *The Student Volunteer Army confronts layers of silt and sand caused by liquefaction in the Christchurch suburb of Burwood.* PHOTO: DEREK FLYNN

RIGHT: *Smoko time — Olivier Dercq, a member of the Student Volunteer Army, discovers a moment of relaxation during the clean-up operation.*
PHOTO: CRAIG SIMCOX

Chris Moore

Dust and Mud

LEFT: *Silty mud and water swamped Christchurch after the earthquake. This aerial view of Pages Road and Anzac Drive in the eastern suburbs, taken within hours of the 12.51 tremor, provides a vivid image of the extent of the damage. The Avon River is at the right of the picture.*

PHOTO: DON SCOTT

ABOVE: *The city's suburbs were severely damaged. This home in Birch Street, Bexley, lies open to the elements.*

PHOTO: KIRK HARGREAVES

Science defines it as 'a phenomenon when a saturated soil substantially loses strength and stiffness in response to an applied stress, usually earthquake shaking or other sudden change in stress condition, causing it to behave like a liquid'.

Cantabrians know quite a bit about liquefaction. In fact, they have an intimate relationship with it. In both the 4 September 2010 and 22 February 2011 earthquakes liquefaction became a constant feature of daily life for many, with silty sand bubbling to the surface in a sinister grey tide, swamping gardens, houses, garages and anything in its path, engulfing cars and toppling trees, undermining outwardly solid buildings as the ground failed beneath them.

In its wake the grey ooze left hectares of fine, sandy drifts which were soon whipped into dust clouds by the Canterbury winds and traffic.

This was the stuff of which B-grade horror films are made. But for Christchurch this was a reality. Liquefaction seemed especially malevolent through the city's suburbs during and after the 22 February quake.

As the tremor rampaged through the city and its suburbs, it cut a swathe of tragedy, destruction, dislocation and strangely surreal effects.

The area from Hagley to Ferrymead, one of Christchurch's most diverse wards, became a microcosm of the earthquake's effects. Extending from the central city to the beachside suburb of Sumner, it takes in some of Christchurch's poorest suburbs, such as Linwood and Phillipstown, and some of its most affluent, including Redcliffs and Sumner.

The damage in the area ranged from almost non-existent to total destruction, even within the suburbs. Pockets of Redcliffs and Sumner emerged almost unscathed, while rock falls devastated parts of the eastern hill suburbs. In sections of Bromley and Linwood, structural damage to buildings was low, but the hillside suburbs, noteably, Mt Pleasant, that largely escaped damage in the 4 September earthquake were ripped apart. Avonside, badly hit on 4 September, was once again savaged.

Nearer to the city, St Martins suffered significant liquefaction, with the Wilsons Road New World supermarket swamped by deep layers of silt. Many shops in the area suffered significant structural damage. At Murray Aynsley, the heritage homes lining Centaurus Road lay in ruins, their immaculate gardens littered with bricks, furniture and personal possessions.

For weeks afterwards, throughout the eastern suburbs, roads remained torn apart and coated in dust. Many houses were empty or red-stickered. Some sank or split as the earth beneath them continued to fail. Avenues of Portaloos lined streets which had become highways for convoys of trucks, tanks, diggers and uniformed staff. The stink of damp silt mixed with the rank stench of raw sewage. Once attractive roads which meandered alongside the Avon River dissolved into deep cracks and minor canyons. Most residents did not have power, water or sewerage.

ABOVE: *Many owners of waterlogged homes were forced to remove damaged furniture and fittings. This pile of discarded carpets lay forlornly in Bexley's Valsheda Street.*

PHOTO: KIRK HARGREAVES

RIGHT: *The garden of Wendy and Bob Perry's Kinsey Terrace home was wrenched apart by the tremor.*

PHOTO: PHIL REID

First the muddy silt and water — then the dust. In the weeks after 22 February Christchurch faced a new problem as dense dust clouds clogged the air and made recovery operations even more difficult.

PHOTO: ANDREW GORRIE

ABOVE: *Throughout the suburbs, large areas of roading subsided, especially alongside rivers and streams. Peter Kelly of Tasmania, a member of an EQC rapid assessment team, surveys the broken remains of River Road, Richmond.*

PHOTO: JOHN BISSET

SLOW DOWN the Dust is killing us!

ABOVE: *Ray Shearman, 81, and dog, Jess, survey the mounds of muddy silt in the garden of his Bexley home.* PHOTO: ANDREW GORRIE

OPPOSITE: *As dust continued to plague Christchurch, Ronny Graham tries to slow traffic down in Avonside in an attempt to reduce the amount of airborne silt.* PHOTO: CRAIG SIMCOX

In the hours and days following 22 February, more than 300 people from the eastern suburbs sought refuge in the Cowles Stadium relief centre. The centre, staffed by a team of council and Civil Defence volunteers, was established in Christchurch's main basketball stadium. Mattresses covered the floor. Lines formed for the impromptu Work and Income site that sprang up there to help people access emergency relief funds.

Eastern Christchurch resembled a war zone for some time after the earthquake, but amid the rubble the community started to rebuild. Unlike the cordoned-off central city, residents have been able to get busy cleaning.

Hundreds of volunteers descended on these hard-hit streets, collecting and distributing food to strangers. The army also pitched in, with dozens of Territorials called on to shovel silt.

Chrystal Perelini, of Gayhurst Road in Dallington, started food runs to the supermarket, giving away items to neighbours and passing motorists. Her front yard became an impromptu meeting place for traumatised residents, and hundreds of people stopped to be fed.

'We have had so many upset people come through here.'

She said the food continued to flow in, with strangers dropping off bags of fruit and bread.

'As long as people keep bringing food, we'll keep feeding people,' she said.

A few streets away in Bracken Street, Lisa Taylor was contemplating returning to her badly damaged Avonside home, which she

ABOVE: *Someone's home waiting for demolition became a common sight throughout Christchurch. This house was in Woodham Road.* PHOTO: PHIL REID

vacated after the September earthquake. Her new place in Southshore was badly damaged by the February quake. Her old home was arguably the better of two bad options.

Despite the uncertain future, Taylor remained doggedly optimistic. 'We've just got to get on with it.'

In suburbs like Avonside that were hit hard by the September quake, the response this time had been much better, she said.

'I think because so many more people have been affected, many more people are pitching in to help.'

In Seabreeze Close, Bexley, almost everyone had left. The street was badly affected in the September quake and the second jolt was the last straw for many.

Brooke Lush and her family were among

the few who have decided to stick it out. 'We want to make it liveable.'

Like many others, she was helped by strangers. A group from the Living Springs Christian Camp turned up at her silt-covered drive and started digging. 'I don't know any of them — they just came to dig.'

As the team worked, Simon Mutch arrived with his children and a vanload of food. Mutch is the assistant principal at Selwyn House School in Merivale. With the school temporarily closed, he decided to roam the street giving food to strangers instead. 'Now that we are okay, there is plenty of stuff that needs to be done,' he said.

Sumner emerged largely unscathed from the September 2010 earthquake but its luck ran out when the 6.3-magnitude February

ABOVE: *Good sorts — Chrystal and Amo Perelini of Gayhurst Road, Dallington, started food runs to the supermarket, giving items to neighbours and passing motorists. The couple's front garden*

became a meeting place for residents badly affected by the earthquake. Hundreds of people called in for a meal and a chat. Here Amo presides over the neighbourhood barbecue.

PHOTO: KIRK HARGREAVES

Chrystal Perelini, of Gayhurst Road in Dallington, started food runs to the supermarket, giving away items to neighbours and passing motorists. Her front yard became an impromptu meeting place for traumatised residents, and hundreds of people stopped to be fed.

quake ripped up streets and rained down rocks the size of houses on the suburb.

Boulders crashed through the Sumner-Redcliffs RSA and onto a neighbouring construction site where two people were believed to have been killed. Police dug through the rubble for the missing men with their bare hands and with shovels commandeered from neighbours, but later abandoned the rescue effort.

Elsewhere, homes were ripped apart by falling rocks and debris from the towering cliffs. All homeowners could do was salvage what few belongings they were able from the wreckage. Power and water were cut and the main bridge into Sumner was impassable, forcing residents and emergency crews to enter the area via a long, slow and circuitous route.

Many Sumner roads were badly cracked and damaged, making driving treacherous. Shag Rock, a familiar Sumner landmark, broke apart and fell into the sea.

'Sumner is almost unrecognisable,' one long-term resident said. 'It's heartbreaking. We came through the last quake pretty unscathed but this time we've really taken a hit.'

In neighbouring Redcliffs hundreds of residents queued outside the local school to get water. Alistair Kinniburgh was at the head of the queue and was resigned to a long wait and for the exercise to be repeated again the next and subsequent days.

'I think we might be sitting here for a number of days. It's dawning on all of us that this is a disaster far bigger than we first thought. September 4 just pales into insignificance compared with this,' he told *The Press*.

The hills above Sumner are home to some of the most sought-after real estate in Christchurch, but following the quake people there were moving in only one direction: out. While some were being forced to leave by the authorities, many were leaving of their own accord. With continuing aftershocks hitting the area and some hillside areas still unstable, authorities evacuated people from homes judged to be most at risk of further damage.

ABOVE: *The earthquake's enormous power sheared off sections of the cliffs above the seaside suburbs of Sumner and Redcliffs, forcing the evacuation of entire streets and transforming the bustling communities into ghost towns.*

PHOTO: FIONA GOODALL

RIGHT: *The familiar Sumner landmark, Shag Rock (Rapanui) was badly damaged in the earthquake.*

PHOTO: CARYS MONTEATH

'I think we might be sitting here for a number of days. It's dawning on all of us that this is a disaster far bigger than we first thought. September 4 just pales into insignificance compared with this.'

LEFT: *Redcliffs School (far left) lay directly in the path of a major rockfall from the cliffs behind the Christchurch suburb. Miraculously, the boulders stopped short of the main buildings but homes behind the school were extensively damaged.*

PHOTO: DON SCOTT

RIGHT: *This Redcliffs home was badly damaged by rocks and debris.* PHOTO: PHIL REID

Teams of engineers swept through the area assessing the damage.

In Kinsey Terrace, Clifton, Jeffrey Priest was one of the dozens of residents ordered out of their hillside homes amid fears more of the hillside behind them would crash down. The February earthquake had already dispatched a shower of rocks into the back of his Samuel Hurst Seagar-designed home, causing widespread damage and undermining the foundations of the 110-year-old house.

'The back of the house has been wrecked but I thought I would be able to camp in the front of the house. But they told us to get out last night — that it wasn't safe,' Priest said. 'They're worried more of the hillside might come down.'

Sue Moore stood outside Sumner School with her neighbours waiting to get water from a tanker. 'All the Summerhill stone [cladding] has come off our house, the windows have blown out and just about every room is wrecked but we're still living there.'

She and her husband had banded together with their neighbours to help each other clean their homes and get the daily essentials.

'We share food, company and resources and just check on each other,' neighbour Beppie Vaags explained. 'Last night we had a candlelight meal under a chandelier — everything was cooked on the barbecue and it was great. We're all keeping each other's spirits up.'

Much like the many precariously placed houses in the suburb, residents felt like

they were living on the edge. The local supermarket, a community hub, had succumbed to liquefaction and closed. Materials, food and belongings were exchanged without a thought, all for the greater good. The area resembled a ghost town, especially when the silt dust blew. Only instead of tumbleweeds, it was the ancient rock which remained as the only constant.

Across Evans Pass, uncomfortably close to the earthquake's epicentre, two men were killed, crushed by falling rocks on the hillside tracks above Lyttelton. Below, the tremor's force lifted two 1400-tonne Lyttelton Port cranes off the ground and out of their rails and twisted massive wharf piles like cardboard.

Elsewhere in the town, Wendy Souter was playing the piano in the 141-year-old Holy Trinity Anglican Church when the windows imploded and the wall beside the piano collapsed. She survived, unscathed but deeply shocked.

Across the street the stout walls of St Joseph's Catholic Church disintegrated, while

ABOVE: *The tremor shattered tiled roofs throughout the Christchurch suburbs, including these Sumner homes.*

PHOTO: PHIL REID

ABOVE: *A damaged house in Dallington.*

PHOTO: ROSS GIBLIN

Lyttelton's old Presbyterian church with its elegant broach spire tumbled to the ground in a chaos of rubble and twisted metal and broken slate. The Timeball Station, the port's unofficial symbol since 1876, became a gutted wreck — stone, wood and other wreckage spewing down the steep hillside.

Elaine Couch's Rapaki Bay home was destroyed by two massive boulders cannoning down the steep flanks of the guardian peak above the small settlement,

Te Poho o Tamatea (the breast of Tamatea). One went through the roof, destroying her kitchen, while a second went through a window, smashing a wall before landing in her bedroom. A third boulder went through her nephew's next-door home, effectively destroying the building.

Through Christchurch and its concentrated web of old and new suburbs, for the city's diverse communities, nothing would ever be the same again.

LEFT: *At the small Lyttelton Harbour community of Rapaki, a car-sized boulder crashed down the steep hillside and through this home, carving out a deep gouge in what moments before the earthquake had been a sunny garden above the sea.*

PHOTO: JOHN KIRK-ANDERSON

OPPOSITE: *The road between Sumner and Lyttelton over Evans Pass was blocked by rock falls.*

PHOTO: DON SCOTT

RIGHT: *Built in 1876, architect Thomas Cane's Lyttelton Timeball Station was not only one of the world's few surviving timeball stations, it was a treasured Lyttelton landmark. But the 22 February earthquake didn't spare the historic building.*

PHOTO: FIONA GOODALL

WATER AND FOOD

LEFT: *In Rangiora Jayne Rattray (centre) and Ben Walker of Heli Contrax took charge of loading food and water for the flight to New Brighton. Based at the Southbrook Rugby Club, hot food and foodstuffs were taken to the suburb by helicopter, cutting out a two-hour road trip along earthquake-damaged roads.*
PHOTO: DON SCOTT

RIGHT: *Sumner resident Beppie Vaags samples the water from a tanker stationed in Colenso Street.*
PHOTO: PHIL REID

ABOVE: *Patience became a virtue in the days following the earthquake as shown by these people waiting for water supplies at Redcliffs School.* PHOTO: IAIN MCGREGOR

Press in Emergency

Chris Moore

PHOTO: RICHARD COSGROVE

As *Press* staff huddled outside the shattered Press building in those first traumatic minutes after the earthquake, any thoughts of the next day's edition were probably far from their minds.

Throughout its 150-year history, *The Press* had rarely, if ever, missed a beat but a violent 20-second tremor now seemed to have brought the newspaper to its knees. The Press building — a Cathedral Square landmark since its completion in 1909 — had suffered severe damage as the roof collapsed onto its third floor. A number of staff members lay trapped in the heritage building as Fairfax South Island regional manager Andrew Boyle led a search and rescue operation. Their colleagues would later be told that one,

Adrienne Lindsay, had died.

As the dust cleared and the aftershocks continued, reporters, photographers and company management began to gather the details of the tragic events, feeding a flow of stories into online bulletins on the Stuff website and working towards the following day's edition of *The Press* by filing their stories through Wellington's *Dominion-Post*. It was soon clear that the situation presented major logistical and human challenges. This disaster was no remote news event: it was one which directly and personally affected every member of the paper's team. *The Press* family had now become part of the news.

Once a roll call of staff was taken, editor

RIGHT: *Doug Whitla helps evacuate staff to safety via Press Lane.*

PHOTO: JOHN KIRK-ANDERSON

Andrew Holden and deputy editor Coen Lammers began to dispatch news teams throughout Christchurch. Reporters and photographers spread through the central city and suburbs gathering information from officials, interviewing eyewitnesses and reporting. For some, news gathering now involved helping the injured. For everyone, thoughts of family and friends haunted their minds.

For even the most seasoned of *Press* journalists, the tools of a professional lifetime had disappeared in the rubble and debris.

Most had left notebooks, tape recorders and pens behind during the evacuation of the building. Photographers' equipment remained in the illustrations department. News gathering was now a question of using ingenuity and resourcefulness to draw the threads of the stories together. Notebooks and pens were shared, begged or borrowed. Once networks were restored, cell phones and texting became essential.

Some reporters found themselves resorting to old journalistic habits as they dictated stories over fragile phone links,

OPPOSITE: *A temporary newsroom in Latimer Square.*

PHOTO: RICHARD COSGROVE

LEFT: Press *Editor Andrew Holden at work at* The Press's *print site at Logistics Drive.*

PHOTO: PETER MEECHAM

BELOW: *Another earthquake, another newsroom at Logistics Drive.*

PHOTO: PETER MEECHAM

reading from hastily scribbled notes.

Meanwhile, an emergency newsroom was established at *The Press*'s printing plant near Christchurch Airport. The plant had housed *Press* journalists after the Boxing Day aftershocks. Now the editorial department returned as the staff cafeteria became a temporary newsroom.

With limited production capacity, sub-editors at *The Press*'s sister paper, *The Dominion-Post* in Wellington, combined with other Fairfax NZ staff around the country to produce a newspaper for the following day.

With a mixture of professionalism, improvisation and determination, an emergency edition met the deadlines. As dawn broke over Christchurch on 23 February, *The Press* was being delivered to readers. 'Our Worst Day', read the headline. It was, as one subscriber observed, a welcome miracle in a time of uncertainty; an essential lifeline.

For the staff of *The Press*, getting the morning paper out was, in the laconic words of a senior journalist, 'what we do'.

PHOTO: RICHARD COSGROVE

THE PROMISE

Rescue work underway on the roof of the Press building.

PHOTO: DON SCOTT

LEFT: *Tim Cronshaw*

PHOTO: DAN TOBIN

The Press's farming editor, Tim Cronshaw, was in the newspaper's cafeteria when the earthquake struck. Three days later he wrote his story.

There's no good reason why I'm alive today. By all the odds I should be dead. The scars I have to show are small — a few stitches in the head, a shoulder that needs an X-ray and long grazes running down my back. There are people who have had limbs amputated, others who did not survive the magnitude-6.3 earthquake. But so easily I, too, could have become another casualty.

I was sitting with a handful of *Press* staff in the cafeteria on the third floor and had just finished a toasted cheese sandwich I'd made for lunch when all hell broke loose. Within seconds of the first shaking it became obvious this was going to be more than a minor aftershock. The walls started shaking furiously and the floor was heaving and buckling. I reached for a steel pole, thinking it would be strong enough to save me when the earthquake reached fever pitch. Behind me another staff member, Lyn Reid, had grabbed my shirt tails and we hung on tightly, thinking we had made the right decision.

Any illusions of safety were soon dispelled. The pole sheared off at the top and the concrete roof and steel beams came down on us as the building imploded. Lyn and I parted company as I was thrown forward, pieces of concrete glancing off my head and a beam hitting me hard on the shoulder. I thought I could make it to the stairwell and dived forwards. I was wrong.

Looking up as the roof came down, I honestly believed I was dead. It was one of the most frightening experiences of my life. The next thing I knew I was in darkness in an area no larger than a coffin.

THE PROMISE

The quake had delivered me my worst nightmare: I was buried alive and in a claustrophobic lather. The dust cloaked my lungs and blood was dripping from my head. My growing panic was only staved off by a thin line of light behind me. I somehow managed to grab my glasses and clean them. Lyn was moaning and we began yelling for help, but it soon became clear this would not arrive any time soon. Other voices indicated we were not alone.

Kicking aside the rubble in the direction of the light, I was able to clear some debris — maybe enough to slither out to the fresh air. I told Lyn of my intentions and that this would mean sliding past her. I can't explain the relief I felt when I managed to inch myself out from under a massive steel cross-beam and into the open. I stood up and looked at a scene of devastation.

The building's roof had compressed onto the cafeteria floor. No-one, I thought, could survive this. Looking down, I saw Lyn and she wasn't in good shape. Her shoulder was smashed, and, worse, her legs were pinned by a concrete beam, held firmly by the collapsed concrete roof and the big steel beam I had crawled under.

Lyn was doing her best to keep in control, but it was obvious she was in great pain. I knew it was useless, but I tried to pull the beam off her. I promised I wouldn't leave and tried to offer comforting words: we had survived and we just had to wait for assistance. I propped up a chair to try to make her more comfortable, but it would have made little difference. To our left in the former cafeteria, we could hear staffers Len McKenzie and Ian Reddington were trapped and calling for help.

The first person to hand was the newspaper's builder, George Piper, one of many heroes that day. George bravely walked across the roof to get to us and together we placed broken concrete under the beams around Lyn to ensure they wouldn't move. Neither of us panicked. There seemed little point. Then a series of aftershocks shook the building and I had to fight every survival instinct not to leave. A promise was a promise.

I was desperate to find out if my family had survived, and was worried particularly for my son, who was at a school with vulnerable 100-year-old buildings. The cell phone network was down but I rattled out text messages anyway. I had to fight tears when the first replies eventually came through and I heard my family were all safe.

George went to help out another staff member in the pay office who was in the same plight as us. Another woman yelled that she was finding it difficult to breathe. All were buried under the rubble. Builders who were constructing the new Press building in Gloucester Street picked their way over a roof to get to us. Somehow Len managed to crawl out between two big beams from the cafeteria to safety. Yet another miracle.

ABOVE: *Two* Press *staff members wait to be evacuated from the wrecked building on 22 February.*

PHOTO: RICHARD COSGROVE

I was desperate to find out if my family had survived, and was worried particularly for my son, who was at a school with vulnerable 100-year-old buildings. The cell phone coverage was down but I rattled out text messages anyway. I had to fight tears when the first replies came through and I heard my family were all safe.

THE PROMISE

The builders concentrated their efforts on Ian and, using a pinch bar, began breaking through concrete. Meanwhile, an engineer arrived with a car jack and tried to raise the beam from Lyn, without luck.

The last I saw of Ian, he was being carried out on a plank used as a makeshift stretcher.

Rescue workers started arriving. One fireman was from Rangiora — I don't know how he got here so quickly.

How Lyn managed with the pain is beyond me. Two doctors checked her and tried to console her. She was in a stable condition. Then urban rescue experts came with specialist lifting gear. One told me it was time to get off the building. I told him I wouldn't go without Lyn. He said she was under good care and insisted I leave. It was good advice, as they eventually had to bring in cranes to lift the beams off her.

With one of the builders I manoeuvred myself over the rubble and headed for safety

ABOVE: *The scene inside the second floor of the Press building following the earthquake. Editorial staff escaped from this section of the partially collapsed building minutes after the tremor stopped.*

PHOTO: RICHARD COSGROVE

When I saw all the buildings down and turned the corner to see the broken cathedral and, behind me, cars staved-in by crumbling shops, I realised many more people were less lucky than me.

ABOVE: *Rescue personnel at work in the wrecked Press building.*

PHOTO: IAIN MCGREGOR

via the new Press building. Nervously, we bridged the gap between the buildings — with the ground many floors below — and had just got onto the new building's roof when the second-largest aftershock hit. I turned around to see more parts of the cafeteria collapse and the rescue workers being shoved around as if they were on a giant trampoline. I thought they were all goners.

The new building felt as if it was going to crack up as we sprinted through darkened stairways and down a ramp out into Gloucester Street. It was only then, when I saw all the buildings down and turned the corner to see the broken cathedral and, behind me, cars staved-in by crumbling shops, that I realised many more people were less lucky than me.

Worse was later to follow when I found out that another *Press* staffer had not made it out. Lyn was badly injured but is recovering.

In
Remembrance

Martin van Beynen

ABOVE: *The moment when a community and its neighbours joined to give each other strength in dark, confusing days.*

PHOTO: ROSS GIBLIN

A day to grieve and pay respects. A day to give thanks and seek comfort. A day to celebrate resilience and take strength for the future. A day to bring races, creeds and citizens together. A day to move on.

The thousands who came to the National Christchurch Memorial Service in Hagley Park on Friday 18 March 2011 came for many reasons and all would, after a hot,

burning day, go home happy they had come.

Anita Graham, who flew from Melbourne to her hometown for the memorial, said it was a 'beautiful' occasion. 'The most emotional thing was when Hayley Westenra sang "Amazing Grace". That got me.'

Graham said she and her group felt more positive after the service.

Making his way home, Willie Daniels

said, 'It was awesome. I think it was bloody great.'

Sam Johnson, organiser of the Student Volunteer Army, agreed. 'It was a very moving service and really lovely to have the prayers from different denominations.'

Urban Search and Rescue Task Force deputy leader Ralph Moore said a prolonged standing ovation as the rescuers arrived in Hagley Park was overwhelming.

'That was wonderful,' he said. 'Just to see the warmth pouring out towards us there. We're all just typical Christchurch boys and don't expect any fuss to be made and for people to applaud us was totally unexpected.'

The service hit the right note on many counts. The speeches were eloquent and inspiring; the music, especially a stunning 'Amazing Grace' from Christchurch singer Hayley Westenra which had some in tears, gave the occasion spirit and colour; and a diverse, sombre and calm crowd made for an unforgettable occasion. The service will be remembered for many powerful moments and touches:

● The silence at 12.51pm. 'Let us be still,' said the Dean of Christ Church Cathedral, the Very Reverend Peter

THESE PAGES: *They came to Hagley Park in their thousands from every part of the city, the region and New Zealand. They sat or stood under the hot late summer sun to reflect on what had been and what might be.*

PHOTOS: LAWRENCE SMITH;
NATASHA MARTIN; ROSS GIBLIN

Beck, and all that could be heard for the next two minutes was the wind in the trees and the generators humming away to keep the power on.

- An impromptu 'Pokarekare Ana' by Westenra and a Muslim blessing for the dead followed by a Jewish one.
- The acknowledgement of Japan and its recent calamity, with many speakers conveying sympathy and thoughts.
- Prince William passing on his grandmother's sympathy, repeating her sentiment 'Grief is the price you pay for love'.

- The lone Christchurch piper, Richard Hawke, before his biggest ever live audience, playing 'Flowers of the Forest'.
- The attendance of Victoria Cross recipient Willie Apiata and representatives of the Pike River disaster families.
- The blast of the stirring Crusaders anthem '1492 Conquest of Paradise' by Vangelis, to highlight the loss of a stadium.
- The 22 New Zealand flags on either side of the stage and a heartfelt national anthem.

ABOVE: *HRH Prince William was the Queen's envoy to Christchurch's day of remembrance. He spoke about love and loss, urging Cantabrians to be strong in the face of adversity.*
PHOTO: MARK TAYLOR

Shortly after his arrival, Prince William was greeted by Ngai Tahu kaumatua and iwi leaders.

PHOTO: MARK TAYLOR

- The standing ovation for Urban Search and Rescue personnel as they arrived.
- A marvellous rendition of 'How Great Thou Art' was started by an unidentified soloist. Everyone in the crowd joined in.

There were lighter moments, too: the clamour at Prince William's entrance and his mangling of 'kia kaha'; the reference by the Anglican Bishop of Christchurch, Victoria Matthews, to quake 'oracle' Ken Ring; the fire in the brazier that failed to flame until Student Army leader Sam Johnson fiddled with something; and kaumatua Henare Tau telling Prince William 'may you nibble at the apple and be fruitful'.

The thousands who attended began streaming into Hagley Park well before noon under a blue autumn sky in which the slogan 'Rise up, Christchurch' flew from a kite. Many families brought several generations and their picnic baskets, cushions, rugs to put on the patchy grass, sunhats, chairs and summer clothes. Canterbury's red and black, often in the form of a Crusaders jersey, was everywhere.

Rangiora vet Sam Taylor said he had donned the red and black jersey to show solidarity. His fiancée, Mitzi Milligan, and friend Vanessa Clements also wore red and black but more fashionably.

Ginny Cairns, who lived in the city centre before the quake, said she and her friends had come because 'we need to be together today'.

'We wanted to pay our respects and we feel it's a moving-on point,' said Lindsey Fagan of Burwood.

Shane and Kathryn Holdsworth brought along their twins Liliana and Elysia, aged seven. 'The city is grieving and by coming together there is support,' Kathryn said.

Grant Harris, a city council worker, had brought along his son Isaiah, aged nine. 'It's important he is here,' Harris said. 'It's a big day for children. Hopefully after this we can move on.'

Andrea Abrams, from Burnside, was at the service with her parents Dawn and John and her daughters Rosemary, nine, and Mathilde, seven years old. 'I'm here to see Prince William and support Christchurch,' she said. 'What a perfect day. How often do we get no wind?'

The speeches emphasised the themes of lamenting the dead and injured, celebrating the resilience and kindness of Cantabrians and looking to the future.

Leading the two minutes' silence, the Reverend Peter Beck said 'we have lost so much. For myself I hold tears of thankfulness for the amazing spirit that is within us. We call it the Canterbury spirit.

ABOVE: *'Grief is the price you pay for love . . .' Prince William speaks during the service in Hagley Park.*
PHOTO: MARK TAYLOR

OPPOSITE: *Confronting the unimaginable — a video of the city after the 22 February earthquake was a poignant reminder of recent experience.*
PHOTO: ROSS GIBLIN

A day to grieve and pay respects. A day to give thanks and seek comfort. A day to celebrate resilience and take strength for the future. A day to bring races, creeds and citizens together.
A day to move on.

It is in the worst of times we often see the best in people and that is what we have seen in the last few weeks.'

He paused to wait for the applause, prompted by a thank you to the emergency services, to subside.

'We are here all of us people of many faiths, people of no faith, but we come in a common purpose. Whatever your faith may be, I hope you will allow the prayers of the church, of many faiths that are here, to be a vehicle for each of you as we mourn.'

The service was 'just another step on the journey', he said. 'Today, as we begin to rebuild our lives, our city, we look to the future with hope and the resilience that has made us the people of Christchurch.'

Prime Minister John Key said the earthquake had 'left scars that will never be erased from our land and our hearts'. The dead were 'faces of a Christchurch that will never be as it was again'.

'We are conscious we are united in our loss with families in more than 20 countries. We embrace them as part of the wider New Zealand community. Your family members have become part of the story of this city and we remember your loved ones as we remember our own.'

Key says uncertainty would make the recovery slow, painful and difficult, but he also wanted to talk about hope and healing.

'From the first moments the response has been tremendous. There are people alerted by the cries of total strangers who went immediately to their aid. The country has rallied magnificently. It goes beyond our shores.'

He paid tribute to the resilience of every Christchurch citizen who had done what must be done.

'They have resisted despair and had the bravery to go on. These have been such difficult days. Here in the beautiful Hagley Park we see a face of a city that is broken but not beaten. Let us today resolve to rise again.

'We need to learn from the tragedy of

ABOVE: *Singing songs of comfort — Cantabrian Hayley Westenra returned from London to join Christchurch on its day of remembrance.*
PHOTO: MARK TAYLOR

RIGHT: *Many came to mourn the loss of family members and friends in the disaster.*

PHOTO: MARK TAYLOR

BELOW: *Corporal Willie Apiata VC joined members of the armed forces at the service.*

PHOTO: MARK TAYLOR

ABOVE: *The captain of the All Blacks, Richie McCaw, was among the community leaders who came to join Christchurch in Hagley Park.*

PHOTO: MARK TAYLOR

February 22 but there are many things we have learned already. We have learned the power not only of individuals but also the power of community. We have witnessed in the past three weeks the very best of human spirit. We have seen the coming together of a city and a nation.'

Prince William, wearing a Maori cloak given to him by Ngai Tahu kaumatua, conveyed the condolences of the royal family.

'My grandmother once said that grief is the price you pay for love. Here today we love and we grieve,' the prince told the crowd.

He also brought a personal message, he said, which arose from seeing the tragedy unfold from afar.

'It is a message about strength through kindness. About fortitude. Courage and understated determination have always been the hallmarks of New Zealanders, of Cantabrians. These things the world has long known. But to see them so starkly demonstrated has been humbling. Put simply, you are an inspiration to all people. I count myself enormously privileged to be here to tell you that. Kia kaha, be strong.'

Christchurch mayor Bob Parker, speaking passionately and without notes, said Christchurch could honour the dead by dedicating itself to rebuilding a place of great learning.

'How do we find a way to make sense of this thing? I look to the families of those we have lost. We have to find inspiration to move forward. Those lives that have been lost have to be given real meaning as this city goes forward. We have to make here in this city a stage, a doorway through which our young and the young of other nations can aspire to the best. We think of the business people. We will rebuild a city in which businesses can prosper and jobs can be re-created.

'In the end, to give meaning to this terrible event we have to have faith in ourselves. From suffering and pain, we have to reach into our hearts and our spirit and our self-belief to build the safest city so this thing never happens again.

'We will rebuild the shattered suburban fabric. We will stand by our people. We will have a city that will again be the most beautiful city on the planet to live. That is our goal.'

ABOVE: *We stood together and faced the storm — three individuals give each other strength during the remembrance service.*
PHOTO: ROSS GIBLIN

OPPOSITE: *Flying high above Hagley Park, this message gave a signal of hope for the crowd below.*
PHOTO: ROSS GIBLIN

Towards the Future

Paul Gorman

When violent shaking caused the Christ Church Cathedral spire to shake, crumble and crash onto the paving slabs of Cathedral Square at 12.51pm on Tuesday 22 February 2011, it should hardly have come as a surprise.

Previous collapses of the Anglican cathedral's steeple have not been as spectacular or comprehensive as the latest, but it is a sobering thought that before 22 February the spire had sustained varying degrees of damage no less than four times after significant or major earthquakes around the region. The worst was following the magnitude 7.3 Glynn Wye quake of 1 September 1888, when the top 8m of steeple crumpled to the ground.

If the cathedral spire has acted rather like a weathervane for earthquake activity over the years, it gives a good indication of the level of seismic hazard in Canterbury. While there was a definite hiatus in ground stirrings across the region after the 1994 Arthur's Pass quakes and until 4 September 2010, the history of Canterbury is one punctuated by frequent damaging shakes.

Since GeoNet records began in the 1860s there have been 95 quakes in Canterbury of at least 5 in magnitude (22 from 4 September 2010 on), 16 of magnitude 6 or more, and three of magnitude 7 or higher. The biggest so far measured was the September 1888 event on the Hope Fault. The seismological elephant in the room is the slumbering and menacing Alpine Fault, which has not ruptured within that timeframe but is capable of generating quakes of around magnitude 8, some 30 times more powerful in terms of energy released than the 4 September earthquake.

The Alpine Fault is a tremendous rent in the Earth's crust that marks the boundary where rocks on the Pacific Plate and the Australian Plate are scraping past and riding over each other, forming the Southern Alps. For much of its 650km length it runs along the western ramparts of the alps, appearing as an obvious straight line in satellite photographs. It begins as the Wairau Fault in the Wairau River valley inland from

Large New Zealand Earthquakes

Notable shallow (generally less than 30km deep) earthquakes since 1848

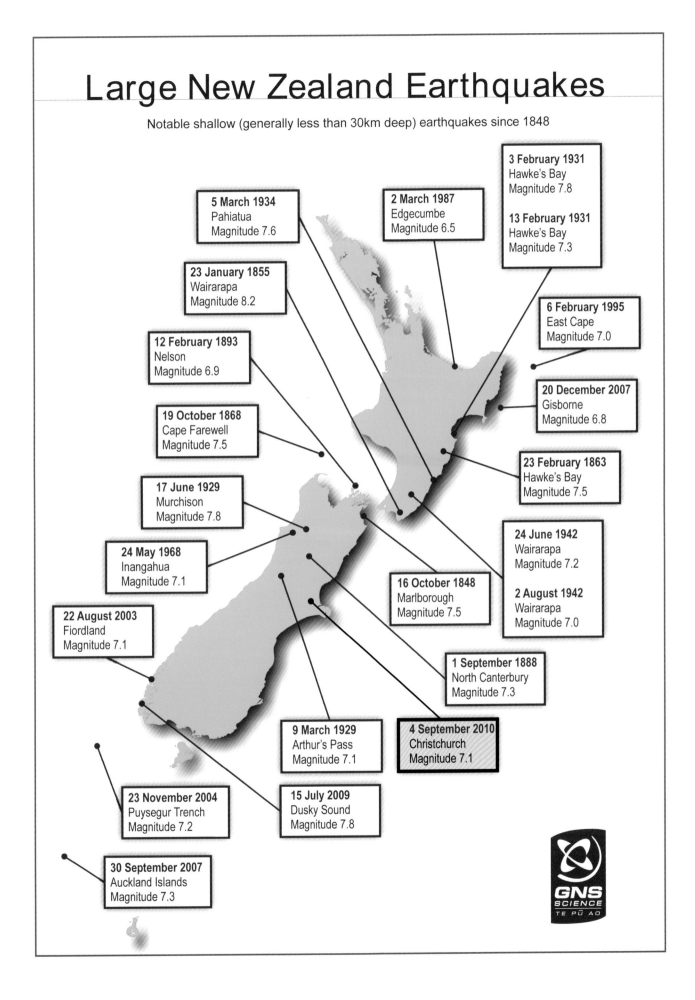

3 February 1931
Hawke's Bay
Magnitude 7.8

13 February 1931
Hawke's Bay
Magnitude 7.3

2 March 1987
Edgecumbe
Magnitude 6.5

5 March 1934
Pahiatua
Magnitude 7.6

6 February 1995
East Cape
Magnitude 7.0

23 January 1855
Wairarapa
Magnitude 8.2

20 December 2007
Gisborne
Magnitude 6.8

12 February 1893
Nelson
Magnitude 6.9

23 February 1863
Hawke's Bay
Magnitude 7.5

19 October 1868
Cape Farewell
Magnitude 7.5

17 June 1929
Murchison
Magnitude 7.8

24 June 1942
Wairarapa
Magnitude 7.2

24 May 1968
Inangahua
Magnitude 7.1

2 August 1942
Wairarapa
Magnitude 7.0

16 October 1848
Marlborough
Magnitude 7.5

22 August 2003
Fiordland
Magnitude 7.1

1 September 1888
North Canterbury
Magnitude 7.3

4 September 2010
Christchurch
Magnitude 7.1

9 March 1929
Arthur's Pass
Magnitude 7.1

23 November 2004
Puysegur Trench
Magnitude 7.2

15 July 2009
Dusky Sound
Magnitude 7.8

30 September 2007
Auckland Islands
Magnitude 7.3

GNS
SCIENCE
TE PŪ AO

The Alpine Fault

Westport ○

Hokitika ○   ○ Hanmer Springs

○ Christchurch

Milford Sound ○   ○ Timaru

○ Queenstown

○ Dunedin

GNS SCIENCE TE PŪ AO

www.gns.cri.nz

Blenheim, heads roughly southwestwards through settlements including St Arnaud and Inchbonnie, crosses the main street of Franz Josef township, skirts Haast and eventually goes offshore on the northern side of the entrance to Milford Sound. The plate boundary then continues southwest under the sea in a subduction zone.

The most active part of the fault is the section between Milford Sound and Inchbonnie not far from Otira. Further north the fault becomes less active because crustal strain and quake movements are transferred onto other faults in the Marlborough region.

Many research hours have been spent investigating the Alpine Fault. During the 2010/11 summer, New Zealand and overseas scientists began an eagerly anticipated, multi-million-dollar project to drill into the fault and set up an observatory at Gaunt Creek near Whataroa on the West Coast. Shelves of academic papers and

Results from this profusion of studies show that in the last almost 1000 years the fault has ruptured four times at average intervals of between 100 and 300 years.

postgraduate theses have already been written by generations of geologists, many aimed at establishing the size and date of previous Alpine Fault earthquakes. To do that they have dug trenches across the fault to examine where layers of gravel and sand have been twisted and squeezed by quakes; used radiocarbon dating to calculate the age of wood in the trenches and of fallen trees; analysed tree rings and pollen; studied lichens; and measured the deformation of the ground using GPS (global positioning system) technology.

Results from this profusion of studies show that in the last almost 1000 years the fault has ruptured four times at average intervals of between 100 and 300 years. The latest quake was in 1717, when nearly 400km of the southern two-thirds of the fault broke between Milford and the Haupiri River, generating a magnitude 8 quake that produced 8m of horizontal movement along the fault and uplift of up to 2m. Earlier in about 1620, a similar-sized quake occurred after the central and northern part of the Alpine Fault ruptured between the Paringa and Ahaura rivers. Earthquake-triggered landslides and damage to native bush indicate another magnitude 8 shake took

OPPOSITE: *The Alpine Fault is the straight line where the snow also stops abruptly on the western edge of the Southern Alps.*
PHOTO: NASA

place around 1450–1460, and there is also evidence of a big earthquake around 1100.

GNS Science believes the fault is now due or overdue to rupture again, with a high probability of that happening in the next few decades. When it does, severe ground-shaking will cause huge damage on the West Coast, with wrecked road and rail links and broken bridges unlikely to be fully repaired for months, possibly even for a year or more in some places. Electricity and telecommunications lines will also be destroyed and massive landslides in the high country will dam rivers and block passes. In Canterbury, the quake will be felt strongly, though not as sharply as the violent 22

February event, and could carry on for a minute or more, bringing down some older buildings and causing extensive liquefaction.

Further north, the Hope Fault also poses a major threat to much of Canterbury. This fault splits from the Alpine Fault south of Hokitika and runs for about 230km in a roughly straight line before heading offshore north of Kaikoura.

The fault has several segments, with the 30km section from the Hope River to the Hanmer basin among the most active. Scientists believe the fault is likely to generate a quake of between magnitude 7 and 7.5 when it does break, with likely horizontal movement of up to 2.5m.

ABOVE: *Studying the past to reveal the future — GNS scientist Rupert Sutherland (left) talks to the media. The Alpine Fault can be clearly seen at the upper left of the photograph.*

PHOTO: AMY GLASS

PHOTO: IAIN MCGREGOR

ABOVE: *GNS Science experts (from left) senior scientist Jiasghun Yu, marine geophysicist Dr Daniel Barker and earthquake geoscientist Dr Vaughn Stagpoole conduct gravity testing between Sumner and Redcliffs.*

Research indicates there is an average interval of only 140 years between Hope Fault ruptures on the Hanmer segment, and with the last one in 1888 the next event may not be far away. In the 1888 quake, which was preceded by several weeks of increasingly strong and noisy foreshocks, 40 to 50 seconds of shaking damaged buildings in Christchurch, toppling chimneys and causing rock falls around the Port Hills and Lyttelton Harbour.

It was also an important event in terms of extending scientific knowledge of land movement caused by earthquakes. Historic photographs showing a section of a previously straight fenceline clearly shunted rapidly to the right where it crossed the fault proved irrefutably for scientists that quakes created horizontal, as well as vertical, motion.

Another structure that needs to be watched very closely is the Porter's Pass Fault, within 60km of Christchurch. This forms the prominent line and associated lumps on the side of Foggy Peak that you can see to the right as you drive up the pass road proper from the Canterbury Plains side. Just below the summit of the pass a swampy area marks the point where the fault disrupts normal drainage patterns. On the pass's western side, the fault trace cuts away to the left to track around the ranges next to Lake Lyndon and continues towards Lake Coleridge, where it has offset

Until 4.35am on 4 September 2010, one of these faults was generally expected to be the source of the next damaging Canterbury quake.

stream channels in mountainsides.

The 40km-long active fault is a prominent element of the Porter's Pass–Amberley Fault Zone, about 100km in length, running along the ranges and foothills of North Canterbury. Scientists investigating the Porter's Pass Fault have found it has produced four to five earthquakes over the last 10,000 years and is a major player in terms of seismic hazard in the region. Radiocarbon dating of organic samples found in trenches excavated across the fault show that when it breaks, it generally moves between 5 and 7m, generating quakes of between magnitude 6.9 and 7.7. Experts always believed a rupture of the Porter's Pass Fault, as the closest known fault to Christchurch, was the one most likely to cause widespread damage and even loss of life in the city. But the good news is, it seems to move on average only about once every 2000 years or so, and last did so between 500 and 700 years ago.

Until 4.35am on 4 September 2010, one of these three faults was generally expected to be the source of the next damaging Canterbury quake. Hidden faults below the sediments that make up the Canterbury Plains and underlie Christchurch are now in the scientific spotlight. So far the September quake has revealed the existence of at least three, possibly four, previously masked faults on the plains. The 22 February earthquake has disclosed the whereabouts of the Port Hills Fault and research is continuing into another fault, roughly parallel to the Port Hills one, that

runs under central Christchurch and out to sea near New Brighton. This fault looks to be responsible for the Boxing Day 2010 quake and other aftershocks.

Scientists have debated whether the eastern end of the Greendale Fault may link up with the western end of the Port Hills Fault. The implication of that would be that the fault could rupture along a much longer length, generating a larger earthquake than if the structure is in two parts with a 'step-over' between them. GNS Science seismologist Dr Kelvin Berryman believes the aftershock patterns suggest at least another two northeast–southwest-trending faults could lie between the Greendale and Port Hills faults.

Retired Canterbury University geologist Jocelyn Campbell also points out that a close look at the aftershock cloud at the eastern end of the Port Hills Fault shows the beginnings of a pattern like a hammerhead: a small line of quakes extending at almost right angles to the fault to the north and south. That might suggest another fault slightly offshore running in a north–south direction. That may also mean more hidden faults with a similar orientation underneath the plains.

Intensive investigations are underway to try to pinpoint the locations of these

OPPOSITE: *The Porter's Pass Fault, marked by the scarp and swampy area in the centre of the photograph running around the mountainside, had previously been thought to be the closest active fault to Christchurch.*
PHOTO: PAUL GORMAN

Aftershocks from the two big recent quakes are likely to carry on, albeit in curtailed form, for much of 2011. And always at the back of our minds should be the very real threat from major Alpine Fault and Hope Fault earthquakes over the next few decades.

ABOVE: *The fault line which ruptured on 4 September 2010 had dramatic effects on the landscape. This hedge line shows the effects of horizontal displacement.*

PHOTO: RICHARD COSGROVE

ABOVE: *A member of Calgary University's Department of Geoscience, Malcolm Bertram, surveys the area surrounding the New Brighton spit following the 22 February earthquake.* PHOTO: KIRK HARGREAVES

underground faults. Researchers are using a range of surveying techniques, including bouncing sound waves off the basement rocks, checking anomalies in the region's gravitational and magnetic fields, and revisiting and refining the locations of aftershocks. Offshore surveying of Pegasus Bay has also taken place. Though preliminary findings indicate there are no previously unknown faults in the rocks below the seafloor, researchers will spend months analysing the data before coming to any firm conclusions.

So what of the future? Are Cantabrians through the worst of it, or are there more large shakes to come? Scientists, who are inherently cautious people, are unlikely to make any definitive statements until they have a large body of evidence to support them. Aftershocks from the two big recent quakes are likely to carry on, albeit in curtailed form, for much of 2011. And always at the back of our minds should be the very real threat from major Alpine Fault and Hope Fault earthquakes over the next few decades.

While there are still hidden faults to find across Canterbury, the threat remains of more unexpected earthquakes to come.

Extraordinary Times

Chris Moore

Christchurch confronts extraordinary times as our city, profoundly reshaped by New Zealand's largest natural disaster considers a very different future (in terms of damage, extent and financial cost, it is classed as New Zealand's largest and for similar reasons it's also one of the world's worst). Every facet of how and where we live has undergone a radical shift. The reassuring psychological and physical landmarks which previously accompanied our daily lives have disappeared or been damaged. The changes to our workplaces, homes and surroundings are now as widespread and complex as the fault lines beneath our feet. We live daily with visible reminders of the disaster. For the families of those who died and for those badly injured, the memories are especially vivid. Christchurch faces a long, difficult journey to full recovery.

The government quickly moved to establish a Royal Commission of Inquiry into both the 4 September 2010 and 22 February 2011 earthquakes. This will be chaired by Justice Mark Cooper, who will be joined by Sir Ron Carter and Canterbury University

Associate Professor Richard Fenwick to examine why some buildings in central Christchurch failed so catastrophically in the February quake. It will also examine legal and best-practice requirements for the design, construction and maintenance of buildings in central business districts throughout New Zealand. The commission will report its findings by 11 April 2012.

At the core of Christchurch's future is a new government department created to manage and co-ordinate the rebuilding of a community. The Canterbury Earthquake Recovery Authority reflects the lessons learned from international experience, particularly Queensland's 2011 floods and the response to Canterbury's 4 September earthquake.

In a situation unparalleled in the country's history, CERA will work with local councils and communities, the residents of greater Christchurch, Ngai Tahu and the non-government sector and business interests for five years. The authority holds unprecedented powers, including the power to relax, suspend or extend laws and regulations to allow faster decision-making on key aspects of the rebuild. It can also requisition land, require information and take over local government bodies.

CERA will have a working partnership with the Selwyn and Waimakariri district councils, Environment Canterbury commissioners and the Christchurch City Council. The Minister for Earthquake Recovery, Gerry Brownlee, is authorised to 'call up and exercise any functions, rights or responsibilities and associated powers, whether in whole or in part, when this is considered necessary from any local authority and council organisation'. CERA can also suspend, amend, cancel or delay any existing local plans or policies.

The Christchurch City Council will meanwhile continue to be responsible for its infrastructure — much of it destroyed on 22 February — while maintaining many other local government functions. It has also been set the challenging task of preparing a CBD plan in nine months. In the words of one commentator, 'it will not want to miss this deadline'.

The establishment of CERA was broadly, albeit hesitantly, welcomed, according to a *Press* editorial shortly after the government announced its establishment.

'No-one who has seen the scale of damage to Christchurch has been in any doubt that effective decision-making will be essential . . . CERA offers a promise with the necessary combination of strong powers and adequate safeguards to give Cantabrians confidence for their future.'

On 12 May, weeks of speculation ended when the former CEO of Orion, Roger Sutton, was named as the man who will lead the city's rebuild. As chief executive of CERA, Sutton replaces Deputy State Services Commissioner John Ombler, who was interim chief executive since CERA's inception. Sutton's appoinment was greeted with almost unanimous support.

'Roger has been an outstanding leader as Orion Network's chief executive, and he has a very keen appreciation of the extent of damage from the earthquakes and need for recovery here in the city . . . I'm sure Roger's appointment will speed the recovery process,' Gerry Brownlee said. 'I think all Cantabrians, and particularly the residents of Christchurch city, can be confident we have found a chief executive who is more than up to the job.'

He said Fletcher Building had set up 15 project offices in Christchurch and had arranged contractors to do more than 4000 emergency home repairs. Major rebuilding work would not begin until the thousands of aftershocks that have hit the region stop.

Fletcher will not be constructing houses in Christchurch, but it will sell material needed to build them, as well as bidding for some commercial and infrastructure work. Ling, Fletcher's chief executive, said the building industry had the labour, resources

'No-one who has seen the scale of damage to Christchurch has been in any doubt that effective decision-making will be essential . . . CERA offers a promise with the necessary combination of strong powers and adequate safeguards to give Cantabrians confidence for their future.'

and capacity after being 'on its knees for the last few years'. The Christchurch rebuild would be a source of 'high-growth' opportunities, he said. 'There aren't that many cities in the world that actually get the opportunity to rebuild.'

The Christchurch City Council faces testing financial times. There were 4108 rate-paying businesses in the CBD before the earthquake, but only a fraction of those can reasonably be expected to be returning revenue to the council again any time soon. On top of the estimated 600 commercial buildings to be demolished, the council thinks around 8000 homes will need to be demolished or significantly repaired, which is a further loss to its ratings base. The $6 million per annum from parking revenue will also be well down and council-owned businesses could hardly expect to be turning much of a profit. Entire swathes of the central city will have to be rebuilt and, eventually, reinhabited.

One fact overshadows everything else: Cantabrians now inhabit a seismically active amphitheatre, one which will largely dictate the city's future. February's 6.3 earthquake is still generating its own sequence of aftershocks, which, according to seismologists, will continue for months, perhaps years. There have been predictions that at least 10,000 homes could be threatened, forcing whole suburbs and communities, especially in the city's eastern areas, to be resited after the ground literally failed beneath them. Some Christchurch hillside streets could also be abandoned as engineers investigate whether they can be made safe from falling rocks. About 400 houses are currently uninhabitable because of rock-fall risk and while engineers continue to examine precisely what areas

remain in danger, it is clear that some roads might never be made safe.

Engineering geologist Mark Yetton said the quakes had loosened rocks, but it would take a wet winter to properly assess the risk to homes and lives. 'Rock fall is not like liquefaction — it actually kills and injures. We have to be very careful allowing people to get back into their homes,' he warned.

More than 300,000 claims have been lodged with the Earthquake Commission (EQC) and $840 million paid out since 4 September. A further 118,041 claims were lodged with EQC following the 22 February earthquake and the 5.3-magnitude aftershock on 16 April, with the commission receiving about 1300 new claims daily.

Fears of an earthquake-driven exodus from Christchurch have meanwhile been questioned by a new study which suggests that, at worst, up to 8000 people may leave the city in the coming year. Estimates soon after the earthquake suggested up to 70,000 people had temporarily fled the city, with some experts saying 4 per cent of the city's population — about 16,000 residents — could stay away for a year. The new report, commissioned by the Canterbury District Health Board, found that population levels were likely to change by no more than 2 per cent in the year after the quake and could even increase as construction workers arrived for the rebuilding effort. Statistics New Zealand figures on school enrolments, however, have indicated that 8.9 per cent of Christchurch, Waimakariri and Selwyn pupils had re-enrolled outside these three areas after the quake.

The human face of the disaster remains etched into the city's psyche. Many residents face an uncertain future, with the closure of a mounting number of businesses and industries

ABOVE: *Seventeen-year-old Christ's College student Geoff Horsburgh plays the bagpipes in front of the Cranmer Centre on Montreal Street.*

PHOTO: ANDREW GORRIE

and the redundancies which inevitably follow. Difficulties emptying chemical toilets and the risk of tripping on uneven floors and paths have made post-quake life tough for the elderly. The young have also been deeply affected by the earthquake: some found themselves in traumatic situations on 22 February, and others faced disruption to their education and family life.

Nothing is as it was or will be again in Christchurch. Its people today confront the situation faced by their nineteenth-century colonial forebears: nothing less than a blank sheet on which to plan a new city.

The process of rebuilding will not be easy. Our collective future will confront us all with difficult questions and new situations which are already demanding innovation, energy, pragmatism and adaptability — in short, the essential components of the New Zealand character.

Christchurch will need every one of these qualities during the coming months and years.

It could take up to 20 years to restore Christchurch after the February earthquake wrecked a third of its central business district, says the head of Fletcher Building. According to Jonathan Ling, the chief executive of the company appointed by the government as project manager for the reconstruction of Christchurch homes after the September and February quakes, there would not be a finite day the rebuilding would be finished. 'There will be new buildings going up in the CBD on empty blocks probably for 10, 15 or 20 years.'

In Memoriam

The following is the list of the 182 victims of the
22 February 2011 Christchurch earthquake.

Dr Maysoon Mahdi Abbas, age 61, Christchurch (NZ citizen from Iraq)
Lalaine Collado Agatep, age 38, Philippines
Dr Husam Sabar Al-Ani, age 55, Christchurch (NZ citizen from Iraq)
Jane-Marie Alberts, age 44, Christchurch
Mary Louise Anne Bantillo Amantillo, age 23, Philippines
Jayden Brytane Andrews-Howland, age 15, Christchurch
Emmabelle Cabahug Anoba, age 26, Philippines
Marina Arai, age 19, Japan
Linda Isobel Arnold, age 57, Christchurch
Matthew Lyle Beaumont, age 31, Christchurch
Dr Dominic Joseph Gerard Bell, age 45, Christchurch
Valquin Descalsota Bensurto, age 23, Philippines
Heidi Julie Berg, age 36, Christchurch
Carey Stuart Bird, age 48, Australia (NZ citizen)
Andrew James Llewellyn Bishop, age 33, Christchurch
Nina Jane Bishop, age 32, Christchurch
Pamela Maree Brien (Pam), age 54, Christchurch
Rhys Frank Brookbanks, age 25, Christchurch
Melanie Jane Brown, age 54, Christchurch
Henry Ross Bush, age 75, Christchurch
Ivy Jane Cabunilas, age 33, Philippines
Yu Cai, age 31, China
Ian Neville Caldwell, age 47, Christchurch
Cristiano Carazo-Chandler, age 35, Christchurch
Helen Margaret Chambers, age 44, Christchurch
Yang Chen, Age 29, China
John Kristoffer Villegas Chua, age 24, Philippines
Susan Patricia Chuter, age 52, Christchurch
Stephen Cochrane, age 43, Christchurch
Rachel Elizabeth Conley, age 27, United States of America
Philip Graeme Reeve Coppeard, age 41, Christchurch
Patrick John Coupe, age 46, Christchurch
Donald Ashby Cowey, age 82, Christchurch
Andrew Christian Ross Craig, age 46, Christchurch
John Barry Craig (Barry), age 67, Christchurch
Estelle Marie Cullen, age 32, Christchurch
Dr Tamara Cvetanova, age 42, Serbia, resident in Christchurch
Betty Irene Dickson, age 82, Christchurch
Joanna Clare Didham, age 35, Christchurch
Jennifer Ann Donaldson, age 55, Christchurch
Paul Clarence Dunlop, age 67, Rolleston

Marielle Falardeau, age 60, Canada
Dian Mary Falconer, age 54, Christchurch
Adam Stephen Fisher, age 27, Christchurch
Maureen Valerie Fletcher, age 75, Christchurch
Ian Foldesi, age 64, Christchurch
Jewel Jose Francisco, age 26, Philippines
Samuel Reese Gibb, age 27, Christchurch
Jaime Robert McDowell Gilbert, age 22, Christchurch
Joanne May Giles, age 60, Christchurch
Baxtor Gowland, age 5 months, Christchurch
Elizabeth Jane Grant (Jane), age 51, Christchurch
Natasha Sarah Hadfield, age 38, Kaiapoi
Yuki Hamasaki, age 23, Japan
Xiling Han, age 25, China
Tamara Lia Harca, age 59, Romania, resident in Christchurch
Jayden Harris, age 8 months, Christchurch
Yuki Hasumoto, age 22, Japan
Yumiko Hata, age 29, Japan
Miki Hayasaka, age 37, Japan
Wen He, age 25, China
Jen/Jin Hii, age 34, Malaysia
Yuko Hirabayashi, age 28, Japan
Yoshiko Hirauchi, age 61, Japan
Marion Isabella McKirdy Hilbers, age 49, Christchurch
Christopher Grant Homan, age 34, Christchurch
Amanda Jane Hooper, age 30, Rolleston
Megumi Horita, age 19, Japan
Hifumi Hoshiba, age 41, Japan
Siwen Huo, age 28, China
Haruki Hyakuman, age 27, Japan
Rika Hyuga, age 30, Japan
Toshiko Imaoka, age 34, Japan
Gabi Ingel, age 22, Israel
Thanydha Intarangkun, age 36, Thailand
Tomoki Ishikuro, age 19, Japan
Kyle Brandon Jack-Midgley, age 27, Christchurch
Man Jin, age 26, China
Kayo Kanamaru, age 19, Japan
Kyoko Kawahata, age 20, Japan
Beverley Faye Kennedy, age 60, Christchurch
Saori Kikuda, age 19, Japan

Yasuhiro Kitagawa, age 39, Japan

Chang Lai, age 27, China

Wai Fong Lau, age 87, Christchurch

Hsin Hung Lee, age 32, Taiwan

Normand Lee, age 25, Christchurch

Jinyan Leng, age 30, China

Ofer Levy, age 22, Israel

De Li, age 18, China

Wanju Li, age 44, China

Xia Li, age 42, China

Phimphorn Liangchuea, age 41, Thailand

Adrienne Isobel Lindsay, age 54, Christchurch

Haruthaya Luangsurapeesakul, age 32, Thailand

Shawn Lucas, age 40, Christchurch

Scott William Emerson Lucy, age 38, Timaru

Catherine McNicol Lunney, age 62, Christchurch

Donna Merrie Manning, age 43, Christchurch

Kelly Lynn Maynard, age 43, Christchurch

Philip John McDonald, age 57, Ashburton

Matthew Stuart McEachen, age 25, Christchurch

Owen Thomas McKenna, age 40, Christchurch

Teresa Mclean (née Elms) age 40, Kaiapoi (NZ Citizen from the UK)

Heather Marilyn Meadows, age 66, Christchurch

Ezra Mae Sabayton Medalle, age 24, Philippines

Janet Dawn Meller, age 58, Christchurch

Adrienne Meredith, age 36, Christchurch

Ofer Binyamin Mizrahi, age 22, Israel

Kelsey Sinitta Moore, age 18, Christchurch

Emi Murakami, age 19, Japan

Jillian Lesley Murphy, age 48, Christchurch

Melissa Ann Neale, age 41, Wellington

Erica Avir Reyes Nora, age 20, Philippines

Blair James O'Connor, age 34, Christchurch

John Joseph O'Connor, age 40, Ireland

Noriko Otsubo, age 41, Japan

Linda Rosemary Parker, age 50, Christchurch

Joseph Tehau Pohio, age 40, Christchurch

Taneysha Gail Prattley, age 5 weeks, Christchurch

Wanpen Preeklang, age 45, Thailand

Jessie Lloyd Redoble, age 30, Philippines

Deborah Ann Roberts, age 39, Christchurch

Joseph Stuart Routledge (Stuart), age 74, Christchurch

Lucy Routledge, age 74, Christchurch

Saya Sakuda, age 19, Japan

Yoko Sakurai, age 27, Japan

Jeff Pelesa Sanft, age 32, Christchurch

Gillian Sayers, age 43, Christchurch (UK citizen)

Susan Lyn Selway, age 50, Christchurch

Emma Shaharudin, age 35, Lincoln, Christchurch

Dr Allan Alexander Sinclair, age 45, Christchurch

Christopher Patrick Smith, age 48, Selwyn District

Christine Patricia Stephenson (Trish), age 61, Christchurch

Reta Stewart, age 81, Christchurch

Beverley May Stick, age 71, Christchurch

Earl Nicholas Stick, age 78, Christchurch

Neil Glyn Stocker, age 58, Timaru

Michael Stuart Coulter Styant, age 41, Christchurch

Rhea Mae Sumalpong, age 25, Philippines

Yoko Suzuki, age 31, Japan

Te Taki Tairakena (Wally), age 60, Christchurch

Hiroko Tamano, age 43, Japan

Brian Warrington Taylor, age 66, Christchurch

Isaac James Thompson, age 21, Rangiora

Desley Ann Thomson, age 32, Christchurch

Lesley Jane Thomson, age 55, Christchurch

Gregory James Tobin, age 25, Christchurch

Shane Robert Tomlin, age 42, Christchurch

Elsa Torres de Frood, age 53, Peru (NZ resident)

Asuka Tsuchihashi, age 28, Japan

Hui Yun Tu, age 22, China

Yurika Uchihira, age 19, Japan

Amanda Jayne Uriao (Mandy), age 38, Christchurch

Valeri Volnov, age 41, Russia (NZ resident)

Jittra Waithayatadapong, age 40, Thailand

Limin Wang, age 32, China

Tao Wang, age 29, China

Graham Weild, age 77, Christchurch

Joan Dorothy Weild, age 76, Christchurch

Lisa Patricia Willems, age 43, Christchurch

Julie Kathryn Wong, age 37, Christchurch (dual UK and NZ citizenship)

Siriphan Wongbunngam, age 27, Thailand

Murray John Wood, age 56, Christchurch

Owen Morris Wright, age 40, Lyttelton

Stephen Robert Wright, age 46, Christchurch

Paul Khye Soon Wu, age 60, Christchurch (NZ citizen from Malaysia)

Sisi Xin, age 28, China

Linlin Xu, age 26, China

Xiujuan Xu, age 47, China

Ayako Yamaguchi, age 30, Japan

Mina Yamatani, age 19, Japan

Didem Yaman, age 31, Turkey

Caiying Ye, age 27, China

Saki Yokota, age 19, Japan

Gilhwan Yu, age 23, Korea

Naon Yu, age 21, South Korea

Didi Zhang, age 23, China

Hui Zhang, age 34, China

Weiyu Zhang, age 30, China

Yantao Zhong, age 31, China

Xiaoli Zhou, age 26, China

My Story

The Canterbury Quakes

By the numbers

182	death toll as a result of the 22 February earthquake. It includes 181 who died on the day itself and one who died from injuries a few days later. Four other deaths which may be earthquake-related have also been referred to the coroner
21	number of earthquakes in Canterbury exceeding magnitude 5 since 4 September (as at 31 May)
247	number of earthquakes exceeding magnitude 4 since 4 September (as at 31 May)
6016	number of earthquakes detected in the Canterbury region since 4 September (as at 31 May)
3 metres	distance increase between Rolleston and Kaiapoi as a result of the September quake
40cm	height increase in Port Hills after 22 February
564 million	number of hits on GeoNet in the six days after 4 September
86	number of heritage buildings to be demolished (as at 31 May)
241	number of buildings to be demolished (as at 31 May)
12,000	number of properties claims identified as exceeding the $100,000 (+GST) cap
54,000	tonnes of liquefaction silt removed after 4 September quake
322,000	tonnes of liquefaction silt removed after 22 February event
5548	number of vehicles recovered from CBD
305,000	number of claims received by EQC since 4 September